THE ILLUMINATED LEADER

The Illuminated Leader

How Leaders Transform People,
Cultures and Organizations

Robert Boggs, Ph.D.

iUniverse, Inc.
New York Bloomington

The Illuminated Leader
How leaders transform people, cultures and organizations

iUniverse books may be ordered through booksellers or by contacting:

iUniverse
1663 Liberty Drive
Bloomington, IN 47403
www.iuniverse.com
1-800-Authors (1-800-288-4677)

ISBN: 978-0-595-53269-8 (pbk)
ISBN: 978-0-595-63324-1 (ebk)

Printed in the United States of America

iUniverse Rev. 11/12/08

I dedicate this book to my wife Cindy for her never-ending encouragement and support. She is my inspiration.

CONTENTS

Acknowledgements

I would like to thank my talented wife Cindy and my good friend Dr. Samuel C. Heady for their review of this book. I want to acknowledge the men and women of the Ohio Air National Guard. For over 37 years I have served with these wonderfully dedicated people and have learned a great deal about illuminated leadership from them. I also want to thank all of my students who have continually challenged me to learn and grow both academically and as a teacher. All my best to you and yours...Dr. Robert L. Boggs

Introduction

Light is energy made visible. To illuminate is to brighten as with light. When we are illuminated we light up; we make clear; we throw our own light upon someone else.

The illuminated leader generates a very special kind of light. The light generated by illuminated leaders is filled with radiant knowledge, compassion, energy and enthusiasm. The illuminated leader serves as a beacon of excellence who enlightens others so they can achieve their own unique brilliance.

Through illumination we become resplendent and illustrious. It is the illuminated leader who transforms people, cultures, organizations, and even nations. Illuminated leaders such as Mother Teresa, Mahatma Gandhi or Dr. Martin Luther King Jr., are examples of illuminated leaders who found and shared their own light and used it to brighten the world.

The illuminated leader models leadership behaviors and traits designed to specifically affect the enlightenment of others. And what are these behaviors and traits that lead to illumination in the workplace? They are *courage, transformation, communication, character, inspiration, service and relationships.*

Courage is a critical behavior for illuminated leadership. We cannot illuminate from a place of fear. We must face our fears and do what is right regardless of popular opinion. The illuminated leader faces their fear and has the courage to make the tough and often unpopular decisions that must be made.

Illuminated leaders bring about transformation. They are the visionaries who see the need for change and innovation. Their benevolent behavior toward others helps create a culture that is resilient enough to deal with the constantly changing world or work.

The illuminated leader is someone who understands how to communicate effectively. They know that effective communication is more about listening than talking. When the illuminated leader speaks their words have substance and meaning that are intended to enlighten the listener. They know that speaking the truth simplifies communication and gains the trust of others.

Character is a combination of multiple traits or attributes that are built over time, are acquired through experience, and make a person distinctive. Some of the qualities of the illuminated leader that define their character include being passionate, exuberate, creative and in harmony with their environment. The illuminated leader's character defines who they are.

One of the greatest needs of any person is to be inspired. The illuminated leader is inspired and inspires others. They know how to bring out the very best in people. The illuminated leader uses friendship and recognition to inspire others because they see the value and potential of others.

The illuminated leader knows that service is important to personal growth and the growth of their communities. They are active in clubs, groups, and associations that add value to their communities. They understand that true success is found in being of service to others. Illuminated leaders serve the greater good with a passionate sense of accountability.

Illuminated leaders build relationships and form friendships because they value others. They bring their unique self into every relationship. There is no difference between family and friends to the illuminated leader. Everyone is valued, loved and nurtured. The illuminated leader understands the relationship they have with themselves is as important as the relationship they have with others. They are energized people who like being with other energized people. Illuminated leaders mentor and network unselfishly as they impart their wisdom for the benefit of others.

Illuminated leaders are the torch bearers of enlightened leadership. The light they produce is positive energy made visible. The light they generate is filled with radiant knowledge, compassion, energy and enthusiasm.

The illuminated leader serves as a beacon of excellence enlightening others so they can achieve their own unique brilliance. They glory in the accomplishment of others. They are the selfless care givers who transform people, cultures, organizations, and even nations. Illuminated leaders share their own light and use it to brighten the world.

1

Courage

"It is curious that physical courage should be so common in the world and moral courage so rare."

—Mark Twain (1835-1910)

"Courage is being scared to death – but saddling up anyway."

—John Wayne (1907-1979)

Courage is needed in the workplace now more than ever. Illuminated leaders are courageous leaders. They face their fears and do what is right regardless of popular opinion. Dr. Martin Luther King Jr. exemplifies courageous leadership. He stood his ground on many unpopular issues. He was mistreated, slandered, jailed, beaten, bombed, stabbed, and eventually murdered, yet he courageously held his ground and was ultimately proven to be a great American hero. His illuminated leadership ensured our civil rights.

We cannot illuminate from a place of fear. Too often we see leaders who are unwilling to make the really tough decisions. We cannot hesitate or run away from the tough decisions or actions that are a necessary part of right-minded leadership. To enlighten we must be courageous. We must face our fears. Courage has many traits and illuminated leaders embody these traits.

Courage goes hand in hand with critically important traits such as *integrity*. Time and again research shows the most important trait any leader must have is integrity. To have integrity means we must have the courage to do what is right, particularly when no one is watching.

There are many other traits associated with courage. Illuminated leaders are *brave*; they have the guts to do what must be done especially when the task is difficult or even dangerous. They show their bravery with a quiet voice. Illuminated leaders have great *conviction*; they take the *initiative* because they are self-assured. The illuminated leader's uniqueness and brilliance are most commonly exhibited through their initiatives.

One of my favorite illuminated leaders was the Antarctic explorer Sir Ernest Shackleton. He was the embodiment of courage and conviction. He earned the undying loyalty of his followers. It took illuminated leadership to save every member of his crew after being shipwrecked from 1914 to 1916 in the Antarctic. Shackleton was accurately described as a Viking with a mother's heart.

Trust also takes courage. Illuminated leaders trust themselves and others. Beginning a relationship from a place of trust decreases the time it takes to get work done and also increases profits. Trust allows the leader to be powerful through the good works of others. Illuminated leaders seldom judge others, they more typically observe their people from a place of *optimism* in order to bring about meaningful and lasting change.

INTEGRITY

> *"Keep true, never be ashamed of doing right; decide on what you think is right and stick to it."*
>
> —George Eliot

> *"A life of integrity is the most fundamental source of personal worth."*
>
> —Stephen R. Covey

Many great organizations such as the United States Air Force (USAF) understand the value of integrity. The USAF believes core values are essential to the very existence of their institution. Integrity is considered to be a timeless value and the keystone of military service. At Lackland Air Force Base, Texas, a "Core Values" video is shown to all airmen attending basic military training. In the video they are told:

> *"We start with integrity because it is the essential element or the foundation on which other values are built. It's being honest with others as well as with yourself, and doing what's right at all times. Integrity remains the very bedrock of the military profession. Service members possessing integrity will always do what's right, regardless of the circumstances, even when no one is looking. They will make no compromise in being honest in small things as well as great ones."*

Integrity isn't a new concept for the USAF. Before it was identified as one of their three basic core values, the men and women of the USAF understood and practiced integrity.

"Return with Honor" is a 1999 PBS documentary that interviews the men who piloted the hottest fighter planes in the world. They found themselves suddenly transformed from the elite rulers of the sky into prisoners of war in North Vietnam. They tell their story of humiliation, captivity, and torture under the very worst of conditions.

One prisoner survived massive injuries despite being denied medical care. He had to lie on a concrete floor in a tiny cell for almost one year as he re-learned how to move his arms and legs. Another prisoner was beaten to death after a failed escape attempt.

A former POW described how he was coached before being placed on public display. The media taped his interview while he defiantly spelled out the word "torture" in Morse code by blinking his eyes.

The moving story of Arizona Senator John McCain and so many others helps to understand that even under the worst of conditions, we still have integrity. The former POWs spoke of how the values they learned through their USAF training helped carry them through years of hardship. When their captivity ended and they finally came home, they truly returned with honor.

> *"When we are talking about integrity, we are talking about being a whole person, an integrated person, with all of our different parts working well and delivering the functions that they were designed to deliver. It is about wholeness and effectiveness as people. It truly is "running on all cylinders."*

Dr. Henry Cloud, Integrity: *The Courage to Meet the Demands of Reality*

The origins of the word *integrity* are seen in the French and Latin meanings of intact, integrate, integral, and entirety. The concept, as explained by Dr. Henry Cloud, means that the "whole thing is working well, undivided, integrated, intact, and uncorrupted." Typically, we look at integrity as *character, ethics,* and *morals.*

One thing we look for in a person of integrity is trustworthiness. For a person to have integrity, they must be trustworthy. Without trust we cannot emotionally connect with the authentic character of a person. There are of course other important character traits we look for in others but trust is at the top of the list. And who do we trust? We trust those who understand us or at least try to understand us.

When we sense that someone really cares about us, we open up and enter into a relationship with that person. We see them as authentic, caring, and trustworthy. This sense of caring applies to family, friends, business associates, and all those we come in contact with. It takes an emotional investment to establish a trusting relationship with others.

Integrity is essential to the success of any organization. The Air Force knew what it was doing when it established "integrity" as its number one core value. Without integrity, critical connections are not made. We are too busy covering our backs, taking care of our own personal interests rather than the interests of the organization. We end up with an "it is all about me" mindset. We lack unity because mutual care, based upon apathy doesn't exist.

Is it any wonder that unemotionally detached, autocratic, antagonistic organizations lack integrity? When you lack integrity, you are setting yourself and your organization up for failure. Again, without trust, there can be no integrity. Dr. Cloud explains that in Hebrew, to trust is to be careless. He explains:

> "It means that you do not have to worry about how to 'take care' of yourself with that person, because he is going to be worried about that too. It means that you do not have to 'guard' yourself with her, because she is going to be concerned with what is good for you and what is not good for you. You do not have to 'watch your back' with him because he is going to be watching it for you."

A person of integrity wants what is best for others. A person of integrity is a person of action who actively engages in right-minded activities that benefit others. A person of integrity is not feared, rather, they are respected. We do not fear a person of integrity because we know they are there for us, they want us to succeed.

People of integrity watch others' backs because it is the right thing to do. Does that mean they ignore our failures? Not at all, sometimes they will intervene if they see us going down the wrong path. People of integrity tell us the truth, even when it hurts. That is what we do when we truly care about others. We help without being judgmental. We help because we care. It is about wholeness and effectiveness as people. It truly is about "running on all cylinders."

TRUST

> "There is one thing that is common to every individual, relationship, team, family, organization, nation, economy and civilization throughout the world— one thing which, if removed, will destroy the most powerful government, the most successful business, the most thriving economy, the most influential leadership, the greatest friendship, the strongest character, the deepest love.
> On the other hand, if developed and leveraged, that one thing has the potential to create unparalleled success and prosperity in every dimension of life. Yet, it is the least understood, most neglected, and most underestimated possibility of our time.
> That one thing is trust."
>
> —Stephen M.R. Covey
> *The Speed of Trust: The One Thing That Changes Everything*

The numbers are in and they are sobering. We have a crisis of trust! A 2005 Harris poll conducted in the United State revealed that only 22% of those surveyed tend to trust the media, only 8% trust political parties, only 27% trust the government, and only 12% trust big companies.

Organizational trust has sharply declined as evidenced by recent research findings:

- Only 51% of employees have trust and confidence in senior management.
- Only 36% of employees believe their leaders act with honesty and integrity.
- Over the past 12 months, 76% of employees have observed illegal or unethical conduct on the job—conduct which, if exposed, would seriously violate the public trust.
- The number one reason people leave their jobs is a bad relationship with their boss.

There are many issues that impact us when cultures lack trust. One of the most telling negatives has to do with the economics of doing business. According to Covey, "When trust goes down, speed will also go down and costs will go up", and "When trust goes up, speed will also go up and costs will go down".

The Enron, WorldCom, and other corporate scandals cost us all dearly. The Sarbanes-Oxley Act was passed to address the loss of trust in corporate America. The consumer has now inherited billions of dollars in costs associated with compliance issues. Factor in the time that is lost dealing with these issues and the penalty we pay is even more staggering.

Mistrust literally doubles our cost of doing business. It takes a great deal of time to look over the shoulders of others. Covey succinctly addresses the issue of the trust dividend by saying:

> *"High trust is like the leaven in bread, which lifts everything around it. In a company, high trust materially improves communication, collaboration, execution, innovation, strategy, engagement, partnering, and relationships with all stakeholders. In your personal life, high trust significantly improves your excitement, energy, passion, creativity, and joy in your relationships with family, friends, and community. Obviously, the dividends are not just in increased speed and improved economics; they are also in greater enjoyment and better quality of life."*

The total return to shareholders in high-trust organizations is almost three times higher than the return in low-trust organizations. Those who have high-trust are more likely to live prosperous lives and to have more meaningful and fulfilling relationships.

On a personal note the toughest question we can ask ourselves is whether or not we feel we are trustworthy. Can I be trusted to keep my word? Have I kept the promises I've made to myself and others? Am I perceived as a person who can be trusted? Do I inspire trust?

We must first trust ourselves if we are to trust others. As Ralph Waldo Emerson once wrote, "Self-trust is the first secret of success…the essence of heroism." To trust ourselves we must have the integrity to do what we say we will do. We must have the inspiration needed to become the person we know we are meant to be. We must begin with self-trust, the one thing that changes everything…then we can trust others.

GUTS

> "Gutsy leaders reject the mercenary notion that their employees are nothing more than human resources, akin to capital, fuel, oil, or machine tools, that can be allocated or discarded at will. Instead, they see people as individuals, with unique gifts and talents, eager to realize their potential. Gutsy leaders aren't afraid of being criticized or even mocked by their competitors. With bravery and vision, they have dismantled fear-based management and replaced it with heart, soul, discipline, loyalty, humor— and long-term record profits. By being gutsy leaders, they have led their enterprises to new levels of performance."

> —Kevin and Jackie Freiburg
> *Guts! Companies that Blow the Doors Off Business-as-Usual*

Kevin and Jackie Freiburg believe great leaders are different even though they have these things in common:

- They are all pioneers, not followers in their industries
- They have a record of long-term success and extraordinary business results.
- Whether they are flamboyant or low-key, they are deeply dedicated to inspiring their people to higher levels of engagement and performance.
- They care about their people as individuals, not just "assets" or "resources."
- They are all doing things radical enough to make you say, "That takes guts!"
- What they're doing can be replicated to help other businesses succeed.
- And they all run organizations we'd want to work in ourselves.

According to the Freiburg's, gutsy leaders have vision and they have the ability to make their vision a reality. They lead by example and they inspire others to new heights of accomplishment. They truly care about their people and they make time to mentor others. They know that power comes from influence more than the position one holds or the title one uses. Great organizations are lead by gutsy leaders who bring about remarkable levels of motivation, performance, commitment, and loyalty. Gutsy leaders are fully engaged, intensely focused, and contagiously passionate.

It was Winston Churchill who said, "The key to your impact as a leader is your own sincerity. Before you can inspire others with emotion, you must be swamped with it yourself. Before you can move their tears, your own must flow. To convince them, you must yourself believe."

We live in a time where gutsy leaders are in short supply. Just look at the debacles of Enron and Arthur Anderson. We see leaders who were all about serving themselves rather than serving the needs of others. There is a prevalent mindset in many organizations that is manifested through a "what is in it for me" mentality." That isn't gutsy, it's disgusting.

It isn't enough to have employees that are satisfied in their work. We need to lead in such a way that our people are overwhelmingly enthusiastic about what they do and why they do it. How can an unenthusiastic leader bring about enthusiastic employees? They can't! Enthusiasm must come from the leader. If the leader's top concern is the welfare of their people, the people will know it and they will reciprocate for the affection and attention they receive.

A gutsy leader understands that the most valuable resources they have are the people that leave their business at the end of every day. It is the gutsy leader's job to ensure their people are eager to return to work the next morning. If people are returning to work strictly to earn a paycheck, the leader is not doing his or her job.

We want our people to see their job as more than just a paycheck, more than just a career. We need our people to have so much enthusiasm about their jobs that they see their work as a calling. When people see their job as a calling, they aren't counting the days to retirement or the hours until the end of the workday or the workweek. They enthusiastically embrace their work. They know what they do has value and that their efforts are meaningful and are appreciated by leadership.

We need gutsy leaders now more than ever. We need leaders who can fully engage our people in the mission, vision and goals of our organizations. In our competitive world, every mind must be fully engaged if we are going to succeed. Our future successes begin and end with our commitment to our greatest resources, our people.

EISENHOWER

Dwight David Eisenhower never led a single soldier into battle prior to World War II yet he was named as supreme Allied commander in Europe. No, he didn't lead men into battle but he led those who did. It could be said that the alliance he led was the most complex and difficult in history yet he utterly defeated the forces of Adolph Hitler.

Under his command, the greatest amphibious assault in history (D-Day) successfully landed 156,000 troops, while coordinating more than 5,000 ships and 13,000 aircraft. Eisenhower, a great strategist and tireless worker, oversaw and approved all of the D-Day plans. His ability to think strategically and act tactically made him a very effective leader.

Eisenhower, known as Ike to millions of Americans, didn't possess any special military pedigree. He was the third of seven sons of David and Isa Eisenhower. The Eisenhower family was very familiar with the concept of poverty. Ike was a skilled athlete yet indifferent to school. He didn't stand out in class. Academically he was in the middle of his class and near the bottom in discipline. The Army Chief of Staff, George C. Marshall saw something in Eisenhower when he promoted him over 366 officers who had more seniority.

According to Alan Axelrod in his book *Eisenhower on Leadership*, George C. Marshall selected Eisenhower to lead because he saw in him the following:

> *"Eisenhower was a unique combination of an aptitude for strategy and strategic planning, a talent for logistics and organization, and an extraordinary ability to work with others—to get along with them, to persuade them, to mediate among them, and to direct them, to encourage them, and to correct them. And there was more. Ike was no small-talker or glad-hander. He was all business. Yet he possessed an infectious smile that seemed to broadcast a combination of humility, friendliness, and unassailable optimism, no matter the odds against his side."*

Ike was a servant leader. He used compromise and consensus whenever possible to make the tough decisions that came with his job. He had positional power and knew how and when to use it but he opted for a more participative and supportive style of leadership whenever possible. He uniquely understood that leadership style should be based upon the individual and the situation he was dealing with. Axelrod explains:

> *"Inept leaders labor under the delusion that power and authority are derived from impressive titles and a perch in the corner office. Successful leaders understand that their power and authority consist of the continuously earned consent of those they lead…A skilled leader established "best relationship" with key subordinates and other leaders through the use of a continual appeal to mutual and collective self-interest rather than by relying on some arbitrary hierarchy of command structure."*

A good leader is constantly looking for those who can improve the organization. Good leaders are not naïve, they know there are those who detract from the vision and mission of the organization and are willing to remove obstacles, human or otherwise, whenever needed. Great leaders deliver both criticism and praise in a fair and equitable way. Ike knew when to criticize and when to praise.

He firmly believed that leadership skills could be acquired through study and practice. Axelrod also observed that Eisenhower had a passion for leadership and included in his observation:

"Too many officers, in his view, never identified with their soldiers; they operated mechanically and were too removed from the needs of their troops. Further, Ike was appalled by the behavior of junior officers who substituted screaming and, on occasion, physical abuse of subordinates for positive leadership. A quotation often attributed to Ike reflected this concern: "You don't lead by hitting people over the head; that's assault, not leadership."

Everyone who knew and worked with Ike Eisenhower identified cheerful optimism as one of his key leadership traits. During the Battle of the Bulge (a surprise German winter offensive in the Ardennes) in 1944, he gathered his top commanders to tell them, "The present situation is to be regarded as one of opportunity to us and not of disaster," and there will be only cheerful faces at this conference table." Eisenhower was both a realist and an optimist. These traits served him well as the Allied commander in Europe. Ike literally converted pessimism into optimism. The result was an Allied victory that hastened the fall of the German military.

Ike Eisenhower serves as a model of balanced leadership. He was a leader who knew when to be directive, participative, supportive, and even charismatic. He knew when to reward and when to punish. His efforts to bring together a diverse team of leaders in the greatest struggle of the twentieth century are proof of his great leadership abilities.

CONVICTION

When I think of Conviction, I think of Joshua Lawrence Chamberlain. Major General Chamberlain served in over twenty engagements representing the most ferocious fighting of the American Civil War. The engagements included: Fredericksburg, Chancellorsville, Gettysburg, Spotsylvania, Cold Harbor, Petersburg and Five Forks. During the war he was wounded six times and two of these were nearly fatal. He led his regiment to fame and glory with his epic struggle to defend Little Round Top at Gettysburg. His heroic actions at the battle resulted in his being awarded the highest honor our nation can bestow upon a member of the armed forces, the coveted Medal of Honor.

Every year on the anniversary of the Battle of Gettysburg I get together with a few of my friends to commemorate the battle that turned the tide of the Civil War. We gather at my house to share food, companionship, and Civil War stories. While he was alive, one of my neighbors, a Korean War

Veteran, came every year wearing his Union hat from when he was a Civil War re-enactor.

After some lighthearted conversation, we settle in to watch the movie Gettysburg. The movie Gettysburg is based on the Pulitzer Prize winning novel *The Killer Angels* by Michael Shaara. I love the book and the characters that are so expertly portrayed in the movie. Watching the movie with my friends has become a very enjoyable tradition.

My favorite character is Colonel Joshua Lawrence Chamberlain. His brother, a junior officer, insists on calling him "Lawrence" even though the Colonel repeatedly asks him not to (doesn't want anyone to get the idea that there is favoritism in his unit). His First Sergeant, Buster Kirlain calls him "Colonel, darlin." You can tell they all care very much for each other. It is the type of caring that comes when you've come to know and love someone because of the type of person they are and experiences you've shared with them.

Chamberlain is a bit of an oddity as a Union officer because he was a professor of rhetoric at Bowdoin College rather than a West Pointer. The college refused to release him to fight in the war so in the summer of 1862 he requested a sabbatical for study in Europe. He then immediately headed to the office of the Governor of Maine where he received a commission in the 20th Regiment of Infantry, Maine Volunteers.

Colonel Chamberlain is the type of officer you would willingly follow. Not because you have to, but because you want to. He is knowledgeable, compassionate, a great communicator, and he cares deeply for his people. He insists on walking when they walk (even though Sergeant Kirlain insists he should ride the horse the Army provided for him), eating after they eat, and leading from the front; always from the front.

Every year I wait in anticipation for his speech to a group of Maine men that deserted from the army due to a misunderstanding on their term of enlistment. Colonel Chamberlain was given orders that authorized him to take whatever action he felt was necessary to handle the prisoners. His words to these men inspire me every time I hear them. His inspiring speech, taken from "The Killer Angels" to the Maine men begins as follows:

> *"I've been ordered to take you men with me. I've been told that if you don't come I can shoot you. Well, you know I won't do that. Not Maine men. I won't shoot any man who doesn't want this fight. Maybe someone else will, but I won't. So that's that."*

General Ulysses S. Grant so admired Joshua Lawrence Chamberlain, he designated him to receive the first flag of surrender at Appomattox Courthouse, April 12, 1865. He was chosen to receive the formal surrender of arms and colors of the Confederate Army. At that time he rendered one of the most memorable and gallant acts of the war by giving a final salute to the soldiers of the Confederacy as they laid down their arms. Chamberlain closed the war in a most fitting manner, by leading the Grand Review of the Army of the Potomac down Pennsylvania Avenue in Washington.

It was Chamberlain's conviction that gave him the courage he needed to lead the Maine men. His conviction to a noble cause and his ability to express his feelings with emotion ensured both his success as a leader and the loyalty and reverence of his followers.

POWER

"Power is not a new phenomenon, it forms the foundations of government, sociology, psychology, history, religion, and the many disciplines that study how people live and work together, influencing each other. It can be intriguing, because power can be surprisingly complex. It can be enticing, because power can be seductive. But it can also inspire and uplift and exalt, because power can be used to help people accomplish marvelous things."

—Blaine Lee
The Power Principle: Influence with Honor

We have the ability to influence others for good or evil. The path we take can be one of honor and respect for others or something less desirable. The leader who follows the honorable path has made a choice to have power through, rather than over others.

Who are the leaders you most admire? Were they powerful people? Did they use their power wisely? Was their power used to coerce or support others? Some of the most powerful people in the world didn't think of themselves as powerful, they just were.

Power can also be deferred, resulting in powerlessness. By ostracizing ourselves from others, we are removed from potential relationships. It is our relationship with others that determines our power or powerlessness.

As children we felt very powerful. Children are uninhibited free spirits who are greatly influenced by authority figures. Over time, just as the mountains are worn down by adverse weather, people are worn down by adverse comments. Self-doubt is not a natural state of being. Self-doubt is learned over time.

The world is full of teachers who are experts on lessons in powerlessness. Yet who among us would sign up for such a course? But the classrooms are full and the lessons continue throughout life. Who do you think you are? What makes you think you're so special? That's the dumbest thing I've ever heard!

Powerlessness is learned and it can be unlearned. Blaine Lee shares the following:

"The capacity to move from a position of powerlessness comes as we realize that we always have a choice. Though we may feel trapped or helpless, we can choose the attitude with which we face our challenges. If we take on the victim mentality and assume there is nothing we can do, we will never gain power. We will live what Henry David Thoreau termed, "lives of quiet desperation."

Some people are deeply embedded in relationships that are mutually beneficial while others are not. Some find it hard to enter into relationships even when they desire to be with others. Power comes to a person when they understand the importance of positive relationships and are willing to commit to and influence others for the right reasons.

Mahatmi Gandhi understood what power is really all about. He did not fit most peoples image of what a powerful person would look or act like. As a schoolboy he was shy. He was an average student. When he studied to be a lawyer he would become speechless in public or even before a small group of people. He was not a physically imposing person. Gandhi was drawn to people. He identified with their personal circumstances and behaviors. He acted on behalf of others even when it meant he would suffer the consequences of his actions. He listened attentively to the humblest of people. He walked through slums, uplifted the oppressed with great benevolence.

Gandhi understood the importance of relationships. He was committed to a cause and was willing to spend over seven years in prison because he cared about people. Gandhi explained power this way: "Power based on love is a thousand times more effective and permanent than the one derived from fear of punishment."

What we see in many organizations today is fear based power. What Gandhi exemplified was love based power. Even though he carried no official title or held any official position, Gandhi was very powerful. Through passive resistance he was able to free a nation. That is power!

Being powerful or powerless is a choice. Choose wisely, either decision carries certain responsibilities and outcomes with far reaching effects. I hope you choose to be powerful. Be powerful the way Gandhi was powerful, through and for the good of others.

SELF-EMPOWERMENT

"Our deepest fear is not that we are inadequate. Our deepest fear is that we are powerful beyond measure. It is our light, not our darkness, that most frightens us. We ask ourselves, who am I to be brilliant, gorgeous, talented, fabulous? Actually, who are you not to be? You are a child of God. Your playing small doesn't serve the world. There is nothing enlightened about shrinking so that other people won't feel insecure around you. We are all meant to shine, as children do. We were born to make manifest the

glory of God that is within us. It's not just in some of us; it's in everyone. And as we let our own light shine, we unconsciously give other people permission to do the same. As we're liberated from our own fear, our presence automatically liberates others."

—Marianne Williamson
A Return to Love: Reflections on the Principles of a Course in Miracles

The first time I heard the words of Marianne Williamson was during a scene from the movie *Coach Carter*. In the movie, a troubled young man had been asked what his greatest fear was by his coach. I was surprised when I finally heard his answer. I thought he might say he was afraid of failure, injury, death, some inadequacy. Instead, I heard him utter the words of Marianne Williamson. I heard this person say his deepest fear was that he was powerful beyond measure.

It wasn't until I read Dr. Stephen Covey's book, *The 8th Habit: From Effectiveness to Greatness* that I discovered the true source of these thought provoking words. Marianne Williamson certainly had a different way of looking at the concept of power.

There are many types of power. We know that some individuals have positional power. Their power is based on their name officially appearing on an organization chart. Some have power because they have expertise that is valued by others. Some have referent power. They are admired by their followers because their actions and relationships show them to be deserving of followership. Information power is also legitimate and we have all experienced what happens when we are denied the information we need to do our jobs.

Our uniqueness is what makes us powerful beyond belief. It is through our uniqueness that we bring our talents to the workplace and in our efforts to make a difference we fill a void that cannot be filled by anyone else in quite the same way. It is therefore our job, our duty, to bring our talents to bear. Yet, without initiative, our uniqueness will not manifest itself. Without initiative we cannot become the powerful influence needed to make a true difference in our lives and the lives of others.

Dr. Covey explains:

"Taking initiative is a form of self-empowerment. No formal leader has empowered you. The organizational structure hasn't empowered you. Your job description hasn't empowered you. You empower yourself based on the issue or problem or the challenge at hand."

By taking initiative we show the world our unique brilliance. We become powerful as we were always intended to be. It is okay to let our own light shine, and consciously give other people permission to do the same.

Illuminated leaders liberate themselves from their fears and respect others in such a way that they can also be liberated to be the brilliant, gorgeous, talented, fabulous people they are and were always meant to be.

BRAVERY

Lyman Frank Baum (1856-1919) was an entrepreneur who worked in the theatre, newspaper and magazine businesses; he manufactured axle grease and managed a general store in Aberdeen, South Dakota. He was a poultry farmer and published his first book, about raising chickens, in 1886. Few of his enterprises were successful, however; he always enjoyed telling his children bedtime stories, so he turned to writing for children.

His children's favorite bedtime stories were about a land called Oz and in 1900 *The Wizard of Oz* was published. It was an overnight success and allowed him to fulfill his life long dream of becoming a playwright. In 1939 Hollywood boosted the reputation of this wonderful story with an early film starring Judy Garland. Some of my earliest childhood recollections were of watching *The Wizard of Oz* at my grandmother's home.

Many of us grew up experiencing the excitement of what has been described as the first American fairy tale. We remember how courageous Dorothy's dog Toto was when he protected her from the Lion. Dorothy, heedless of danger, ran forward and slapped the Lion on the noise as hard as she could and said:

"Don't you dare to bite Toto! You ought to be ashamed of yourself, a big beast like you, to bite a poor little dog!"

When the Lion exclaimed that he didn't bite Toto, Dorothy retorted. "You are nothing but a big coward." The Lion then admitted his cowardice to Dorothy and her companions.

"What makes you a coward?" asked Dorothy, looking at the great beast in wonder, for he was as big as a small horse.

"It's a mystery," replied the Lion. "I suppose I was born that way. All the other animals in the forest naturally expect me to be brave, for the Lion is everywhere thought to be the King of Beasts. I learned that if I roared very loudly every living thing was frightened and got out of my way. Whenever I've met a man I've been awfully scared; but I just roared at him, and he has always run away as fast as he could go. If the elephants and tigers and bears had ever tried to fight me, I should have run myself—I'm such a coward; but just as soon as they hear me roar they all try to get away from me, and of course I let them go."

There are many people in this world who are in positions of influence who still think if they just roar loud enough, everyone will do what they say.

They think yelling, screaming and shouting at others is an act of bravery. Not true, that type of behavior is cowardice.

Real bravery is shown in a quiet voice. When we take the time to talk with others about our concerns, particularly when we are concerned about the outcome, we are acting courageously. Pounding on desks, slamming doors, diminishing others, are all forms of cowardice. The bravest people I've ever met were kind, considerate, and caring of others. When they had to deliver bad news, they did so with a spirit of compassion.

It doesn't take much effort for someone to be a bully. It does take courage to face our fears. It also takes a great deal of courage to stand up to bullies. I wouldn't necessarily suggest smacking them on the nose the way Dorothy did. A better way of dealing with bullies is to let them know their actions are unacceptable. Don't follow their lead, rather, lead by example. The real King or Queen of the forest is the person who faces their fears and bravely takes the appropriate action.

We remember from The Wizard of Oz that it was the Wizard himself who explained to a rather skeptical Lion:

"You have plenty of courage, I am sure...All you need is confidence in yourself. There is no living thing that is not afraid when it faces danger. True courage is in facing danger when you are afraid, and that kind of courage you have in plenty."

Remember, Dorothy's journey to find her way back home was only possible with the help of others. She didn't bully her way back to Kansas. Instead, she faced her fears while helping a rather unique group of characters successfully face their own fears. Dorothy showed real bravery. She took the time to talk with others about her concerns, particularly when she was concerned about the outcome. She acted courageously and helped to instill bravery in others. She didn't throw tantrums or diminish those she needed to help her return home.

The bravest people I've ever met were kind, considerate, and caring of others. When they had to deliver bad news, they did so with a spirit of compassion.

Together, they bravely turned their dreams into reality.

OPTIMISM

"No other life-form on the planet knows negativity, only humans, just as no other life-form violates and poisons the Earth that sustains it. Have you ever seen an unhappy flower or a stressed oak tree? Have you come across a depressed dolphin, a frog that has a problem with self-esteem, a cat that cannot relax, or a bird that carries hatred and resentment? The only animals that may occasionally experience something akin to negativity or

show signs of neurotic behavior are those that live in close contact with humans and so link into the human mind and its insanity."

—Eckhart Tolle
The Power of Now

Eckhart Tolle goes on to explain that by watching plants and animals you can learn acceptance of what is. Plants and animals will teach you about Being. You can learn about what it means to be one, to be yourself, to be real. Not an easy task in a world that constantly reminds us of the existence of cruelty and suffering.

I've noticed our two cats and sheep dog have no problem being themselves. They don't appear to be stressed at all. They offer no negativity but instead bring our family a sense of joy just through their presence. When they are not eating or sleeping they are playing. Animal's to-do lists aren't very long and their list (eat, sleep, play) makes a lot of sense.

Animals are our companions. Our two cats are my wife's constant companions just as our sheep dog is mine. We can learn a lot by being around them and taking time to observe them. Their world is one of acceptance.

It seems to me that animals accept what is. They are not tormented by the past or stressed by what might happen in the future. Animals are in the Now. Because they are so focused on the Now and being who and what they are, negativity isn't part of their reality.

Animals are free of judgments. They neither judge others or themselves. How stress relieving that would be. Can you imagine a world where we accept others for who they are rather than who we think they should be? What if others didn't judge us but rather accepted us for who we are.

It is a fact that we judge others all the time. Within seconds of seeing or meeting someone we judge them based upon their appearance. Initial impressions center on attributes such as education, wealth, occupation, intelligence, and more. Initial impressions can be lasting impressions that can be unfair yet they are made almost instantaneously and without the permission of those being judged. So, we certainly can't say this world is free of judgment or the negative consequences these judgments can bring.

Millions upon millions have suffered or have received unfair and often times the harsh judgments of others. Maybe if we replaced judgment with compassion our awareness of self and others would take a turn for the better.

So how do we remove negativity from our life? First, it is doubtful we can totally eliminate negativity. We can decrease negativity and the impact it has on us. To do this we can begin by accepting the fact that what has happened in our past is best left in the past. Forgiveness is a strong medicine that at first might taste bitter but the soothing after effect it brings is well worth the effort. Forgive yourself and forgive others, you'll feel better.

The concept of forgiveness is directly linked with judgment. Being non-judgmental is a powerful way to decrease negativity. Take off your judge's robe and spend more time observing what is happening inside you.

Everyone cannot and will not be who and what you want them to be. They will not do exactly what you want them to do. They probably will not meet your high standards but that's not why they are here anyway. Let others

be who they were meant to be and you can then be who you were meant to be. The most important observation is self-observation. You are not observing others in order to change them, you are observing in order to change yourself. Be aware of your emotions and thoughts. Are they positive or negative? If they are negative, think of all the good things you have in your life and rid yourself of negative thoughts. We all have negative thoughts, but to dwell on them is a personal choice that can be changed with some effort.

We can be more like the animals, plants and trees. We can become observers instead of judges. We can replace negativity with optimism. We can learn from the past without being tormented. Rather than being stressed, we can look forward to the future while living full and meaningful lives in the Now.

Action plan for being more courageous:

- Treat life as a learning process.
- Replace hierarchy with stewardship.
- Take personal responsibility for ethical behavior.
- Be a person of integrity in all you do.
- Be a person of action engaging in right-minded activities that benefit others.
- Trust yourself and trust others.
- Fully engage your people in the organizations mission, vision and goals.
- Use compromise and consensus in decision making.
- Deliver praise and criticism in a fair and equitable manner.
- Be a cheerful and optimistic leader.
- Express your convictions to others with feeling and emotion.
- Choose to be powerful through others.
- Show your uniqueness, your brilliance, through your initiatives.
- Show your bravery with a quiet voice.
- Replace negativity with optimism.
- Don't judge others, rather, observe others in order to change yourself.

Reflective Thoughts

2

Transformation

"We must become the change we seek in the world."

—Gandhi

"First comes thought; then organization of that thought, into ideas and plans; then transformation of those plans into reality. The beginning, as you will observe, is in your imagination."

—Napoleon Hill

"The meeting of two personalities is like the contact of two chemical substances: if there is any reaction, both are transformed."

—Carl Jung

Illuminated leaders bring about transformation. The transformation begins with self but can incorporate entire organizations and cultures. The greatest leaders have always been the visionaries who light the path towards transformation. Dr. King, Mother Teresa and Gandhi are examples of illuminated leaders whose efforts and personal sacrifices helped to enlighten the world.

The traits that support transformational efforts are critical to the success of an illuminated leader. Without vision there can be no transformation. It is through the leader's vision that *change* is possible. It took a visionary such as Dr. King to lead the American Civil Rights Revolution. He found a better way, a way of non-violence to make the world a better place.

Change, even in the best of times can be very difficult. Our gut tells us to stay the same yet the one constant in the universe is that everything changes all of the time. The illuminated leader understands the need for and the advantages to change. The illuminated leader doesn't just let change happen, they plan for it.

From change comes *innovation* and through innovation organizations thrive. The illuminated leader understands that innovation is a trait that is required for survival in today's competitive business world. Organizations have to make innovation a part of their culture. The alternative to innovation is irrelevance and that is something no person or organization can afford.

The illuminated leader helps to shape the *culture* of the organization. Culture is who we are collectively. It literally deals with how we do things around here. Is this a fun place to work? Do we respect each other? What do we value? Culture is difficult to change yet every leader must be aware of their organizations culture and must actively tweak it towards the transformation they want to see. Every organization has a culture and it is the illuminated leader who ensures the culture is one of benevolence.

Personal transformation is critical to success. We are all on our own path. That path can and should be one of meaningful growth and development. Organizational transformation begins with personal transformation. Illuminated leaders are all about *personal growth* and development. They never stop learning and they help and expect others to do the same.

The illuminated leader understands they must take care of themselves before taking care of others. This is not an act of selfishness but rather an act of *selflessness*. The illuminated leader comprehends the most important relationship one can have is with self. Once we get that relationship right we can more effectively move on to establishing relationships with others.

Today more than ever, leaders must be *resilient*. They must be able to recover quickly from the many surprises that cross their path. They must remain relevant in an ever changing world. Illuminated leaders maintain their resilience by staying informed and involved with the important things that matter. Illuminated leaders are voracious learners. They stay informed on many levels tapping into information whenever and wherever possible. Illuminated leaders are tuned in and turned on to events that add value to their transformational efforts.

It is the illuminated leader who brings about transformation. They understand that transformation begins with self but then incorporates entire organizations and cultures. It is the illuminated leader who lights the path toward transformation. It is their efforts and sacrifices that enlighten the world.

LEADERS

"If there was ever a moment in history when a comprehensive strategic view of leadership was needed, not by a few leaders in high office but by large numbers of leaders in every job, from the factory floor to the executive suite from McDonald's fast-food franchise to a law firm, this is certainly it."

—Warren Bennis & Burt Nanus
Leaders

Many experts would argue that leaders are born, not made. You might even say to yourself that you could never be a leader because you have to be really great, like Dr. Martin Luther King, Jr., or John F. Kennedy. These are very traditional viewpoints of leadership; that leadership is an unobtainable mysterious quality that eludes all but the most gifted members of our society.

Today, many theorists believe that leadership is a composite of behaviors that can be learned, developed, and used by anyone in working with others to carry out a task. Leadership may mean taking responsibility for some action, taking charge of a situation when no one else is able or willing to do so.

In today's dynamic and fast paced world we need everyone to put on the mantle of leadership. We cannot afford to let leadership be some characteristic reserved for those who hold positions that meet some self-imposed ethereal limitation. Instead, we need to know how we can lead in our own jobs, regardless of the title that is printed on our job description.

The first step in becoming a leader is to reflect upon the characteristics we each feel make up a dynamic leader. To do this we need to think about those people that we perceive as being good leaders. Who do you feel are the greatest leaders of all time? Was it a John F. Kennedy, Martin Luther King, Jr., Gandhi, General Patton, or some other military, business, political, or religious leader? In fact, I would suggest you choose as many leaders as you want. Once you have listed those you hold in high regard as leaders, you should think of the characteristics that made them great. Chances are, if you cross-reference these characteristics, you will find that the really great leaders exemplify many of the same characteristics you value most.

In 1987, J.M. Kouzes and B.Z. Posner wrote "The Leadership Challenge: How to Get Extraordinary Things Done in Organizations." They cited a study of managers in the United States that listed the characteristics we admire most in our leaders at work. They came up with the following characteristics:

"Ambitious, Broad-minded, Caring, Competent, Cooperative, Courageous, Dependable, Determined, Fair-Minded, Forward-Looking, Honest,

Imaginative, Independent, Inspiring, Intelligent, Loyal, Mature, Self-Controlled, Straightforward, and Supportive"

This is a very ambitious list, yet we all look for these characteristics in our leaders. To be leaders, we must also look to this list. One way you might do this is to jot down these characteristics and rate yourself on a scale of 1-5. One being an ordinal rating of "not very" and five being a rating of "very much." How did you rate yourself? Regardless of how you rate yourself, this can be used as a tool for personal development and growth as a leader. If you are managing people right now and you are feeling really gutsy, let them rate you. We all have room for improvement.

Leadership is quite often a scarce resource in many organizations. It is hard to understand why, particularly with the talented people that spend such considerably huge amounts of time at work. It's not as though we've placed some limit on the amount of leadership we are willing to accept. "I'm sorry, we have all the leaders we can handle right now, please exhibit these leadership characteristics on your own time and leave the rest of us alone."

We can all make a difference. We can all lead. The real question is; are we willing to step forward and show others that we have what it takes to make a real difference, or are we satisfied just hanging out?

COWPATHS

Michael Hammer, in a 1990 business article in the *Harvard Business Review*, pointed out that the first three decades of the computer revolution were all about, "paving the cowpaths." That means we have basically been automating familiar procedures.

Paving over cowpaths seems right. It certainly feels good and provides a certain sense of accomplishment. Yet, yesterday's paths are not where we need to go. We need to create new paths, travel to new and exciting destinations. Often, the trip doesn't seem so much exciting as it does dangerous.

If we were being totally honest, we would admit that many procedures within our organizations are nothing more than 21st century versions of 18th century procedures? Cowpaths are industrial era practices overlaid with information era technology.

We like old procedures. They are familiar and very comfortable, just like our favorite blanket, robe, or slippers. Besides, the way we've been doing things works just fine. Right? Wrong! Charles Kettering, a farmer, school teacher, mechanic, engineer, scientist, inventor and social philosopher had the right idea when he said, "If you've always done it that way, it's probably wrong." Thanks Charles!

What happens when a competitor finds a better, cheaper, faster, more profitable way to do something? What happens when a competitor discovers a short cut and you don't? You're on the cowpath and they are on the new path, a better path.

Look at where you work. Are you doing the familiar or are you discovering new ways to enhance performance and allow for needed breakthroughs in your business?

Transformation is what is needed. Many leaders are uncomfortable with the concept of transformation. It is risky being the one who pushes the envelope for change. What if I get it wrong? What if I make a mistake? The better question to ask ourselves is: What happens to me, to my organization, if we don't transform?

It is okay for leaders to be concerned with the concept of transformation. Realistically, leaders take some serious chances when they are championing transformation efforts. Tom Peters in his book, *Re-imagine! Business Excellence in a Disruptive Age*, explains, "Britain's two most potent 20th Century leaders—Churchill and Thatcher—were unceremoniously dumped when the citizenry judged that they'd done their thing. Transforming Leaders…tend eventually to wear their followers out."

We need to transform and we need visionary leaders who are willing to lead the effort. Risk taking visionaries are needed now more than ever. Gay Hendricks and Kate Ludeman, *The Corporate Mystic: A Guidebook for Visionaries with Their Feet on the Ground*, share the following:

> *"Some visionaries may be born free from the tyranny of 'is'. But the rest of us have to break free of it. What is this tyranny? It is a view of the world that keeps you trapped in a limited set of options…When the steam locomotive was new, a breakthrough in technology made it possible for it to exceed thirty miles an hour. With the speed of forty miles an hour in sight, a debate broke out, even in the medical literature of the time. One learned doctor said that it was common knowledge that the human body would explode at forty miles an hour. That's the way it 'is', he said."*

When I think of a person that had an effective vision that touched on many lives, I think of Walt Disney. Disney touched all of our lives. I remember as a child looking forward to watching the Mickey Mouse Club and the Wonderful World of Disney. Bob Thomas (1994), *Walt Disney: An American Original* shares with us Walt Disney's vision for Disneyland:

> *"The idea of Disneyland is a simple one. It will be a place for people to find happiness and knowledge. It will be a place for parents and children to share pleasant times in one another's company: a place for teachers and pupils to discover greater ways of understanding and education. Here the older generation can recapture the nostalgia of days gone by, and the younger generation can savor the challenge of the future. Here will be the wonders of Nature and Man for all to see and understand. Disneyland will be based*

upon and dedicated to the ideals, the dreams and hard facts that have created America. And it will be uniquely equipped to dramatize these dreams and facts and send them forth as a source of courage and inspiration to all the world. Disneyland will be something of a fair, an exhibition, a playground, a community center, a museum of living facts, and a showplace of beauty and magic. It will be filled with the accomplishments, the joys and hopes of the world we live in. And it will remind us how to make those wonders part of our own lives."

Walt Disney was sixty-five years young when he passed from this world. No one questions whether the world was a better place for him having been a part of it. The world mourned his passing. He was called "Aesop with a magic brush", and "a poet-magician who brought the world of fable alive." It was Eric Sevareid on the CBS Evening News that expressed best the feelings of Americans at the loss of Walt Disney:

"He was an original; not just an American original, but an original, period. He was a happy accident; one of the happiest this century has experienced; and judging by the way it's been behaving in spite of all Disney tried to tell it about laughter, love, children, puppies and sunrises, the century hardly deserved him. He probably did more to heal or at least to soothe troubled human spirits than all the psychiatrists in the world. There can't be many adults in the allegedly civilized parts of the globe who did not inhabit Disney's mind and imagination at least for a few hours and feel better for the visitation. It may be true, as somebody said, that while there is no highbrow in lowbrow, there is some lowbrow in every highbrow. But what Walt Disney seemed to know was that while there is very little grown-up in a child, there is a lot of child in every grown-up. To a child this weary world is brand new, gift-wrapped; Disney tried to keep it that way for adults. By the conventional wisdom, mighty mice, flying elephants, Snow White and Happy, Grumpy, Sneezy and Dopey—all these were fantasy, escapism from reality. It's a question of whether they are any less real, any more fantastic than intercontinental missiles, poisoned air, defoliated forests, and scraps from the moon. This is the age of fantasy, however you look at it, but Disney's fantasy wasn't lethal. People are saying we'll never see his like again."

Disney was a visionary who understood the need to transform. Now more than ever we need visionary leaders who are willing to lead transformation efforts. Risk taking is all about leaving cowpaths behind and making new paths that lead to an exciting future.

CHANGE

"People of my generation or older did not grow up in an era when transformation was common. With less global competition and a slower-

moving business environment, the norm back then was stability and the ruling motto was: 'If it ain't broke, don't fix it.' Change occurred incrementally and infrequently."

—John P. Kotter
Leading Change

"Change alone is unchanging."

— Heraclitus

We're lucky enough to have been born into an age of unparalleled opportunity. Or at least we would recognize this age as fantastic if it weren't for one little teensy, weensy, issue we all face.

We don't like change. In fact we hate it. We can tell ourselves change is great, we need to embrace it, and it's good for us. It's the only way we can improve ourselves, society, and the world at large. But the real truth, the deep down in our guts kind of truth we seldom dredge up is that we don't like change.

Change is different and I like things just the way they are. Why don't you change the other guy and leave me the heck alone. Besides, what's so bad about staying the same? I like doing what I'm doing and if you'll just leave me alone I'll be fine.

Life doesn't work that way anymore. Now back when our ancestors lived by instinct and the ability to find food, four legged or otherwise, they didn't have to deal with a lot of change. You pretty much knew which herbs did what. And since you were limited to how far you could walk, the terrain didn't change all that much and you didn't have a whole lot of strangers showing up with new and exciting ideas to mess up the way you did things.

When I watch a movie or read a book about hunter-gatherers I want to cry out "for crying out loud, will one of you invent a bow and arrow or something so you can catch something to eat." Let's face it; they were primarily concerned with surviving from one day until the next. Luckily, our ancestors were able to adapt to change when it came along. I'm sure Uncle Og or Auntie Oog didn't much like change, but they dealt with it. I hate to think of what happened to the person that initially came up with the idea for the bow and arrow, growing crops or domesticating animals.

After thousands and thousands and thousands and thousands of years of surviving one meal at a time some one got creative and figured out that if you planted seeds at just the right time, and if you stayed in a location long enough, you could grow food. Storage was still a bit of a problem but it beat chasing down a deer or antelope when your ribs were showing. And although I'm sure the idea of agriculture was very stressful to some hunter-gatherers, the idea of being able to eat, particularly when there were no animals to chase down, was very appealing. In fact, over another few thousands and thousands of years or so, people probably even began to wander what the big deal was. Agriculture was good and we probably should have been doing this all along. In fact, I'm sure more than one egomaniac took credit for it.

A few thousand years later, some pretty bright people started to think up ways to produce and cultivate more food. They began building machines that allowed mankind to reap the fruits that come from an economy that was slowly but steadily moving them towards industrialization. Now I'm pretty sure there were a lot of people that observed the phenomenon of industrialization, such as the Luddites, that cringed at the idea of the changes it would bring about and in these changes, would destroy the way of life they had come to accept, and even embrace. Does this sound familiar?

Industrialization brought with it a mindset that viewed people more as machines or machine parts rather than as human beings. Just like the hunter-gatherers and their offspring saw the world from perspectives that mirrored the natural world that they were a part of, the people from the industrial age tended to see people and the world in mechanistic ways. It was the model they used in order to see the world.

There are thoughtful writers such as Mathew Fox, *The Reinvention of Work*, who helps us understand why we are seeing so many changes taking place in the world of work as we complete our journey through the Information Age and on into what the Nomura Institute labeled the Fourth Era of Economic Development, the Era of Creativity.

Many consider the launching of Sputnik as the starting point of the Information Age. For the first time we were capable of communicating on a global scale. And from those simple beginnings, look at where we are now. I paid nearly $2,000 for one of the first Apple II computers. I hooked it up with a modulator to a TV set and I used a tape player to load extremely phenomenal programs like Pong or Star Trek to a system that had an unbelievable 16K of memory. You can buy a great system today for a lot less than I paid for my Apple many years ago. It makes me want to weep when I think of the changes I've seen since choosing the doorstop I once called my computer.

Is it any wonder that people are stressed? Let me repeat what I said earlier. We don't like change! We never have, and I doubt that human beings will ever be able to say they really do without gritting their teeth and breaking out in a cold sweat. We have to learn to embrace change. Doing things the way we always have just won't get it anymore. Change appears to be moving along at the speed of light. And it will continue to do so until someone discovers something faster.

All of this information technology has moved us into an era that didn't take thousands of years to occur. In fact, what use to take thousands of years has taken place in just the time I've been on this planet. And if that isn't some really serious change I'd like to know what is.

My kids couldn't believe I use to watch television in black and white. When my son was 8 years old he literally refused to watch black and white television. He thought the world use to be black and white and only recently did we all appear to be in color. When I went to England many years ago I thought I was being hurled head-first into the twilight zone. Just like when I was a kid, you could only get three channels and two of them were the same. Stores didn't stay open in the evenings, except for pubs, and what they did offer wasn't worth sticking around for anyway. Choices were very limited.

I'm telling you, things have changed. When viewed from a historical perspective, we've leaped thousands of years in just a few decades. No wonder we're a little bit confused and daunted by the occurrence of events in our lives. We've been impacted at home, at work, and at play

At home I can get hundreds of channels on one of four television sets. I've been informed we need another one in the family room, four isn't enough. My telephone has more mailboxes than the local post office. And my home fax machine is also a phone, a printer, a scanner and a copier.

At work and at home, I get e-mail, voice-mail, and oh yes, mail. Where I use to have a typewriter (ask a Baby Boomer), I now use Word, Excel, Access, Outlook and PowerPoint. The only time I see a typewriter anymore is while visiting a museum. I still haven't mastered all the uses of the computer. The term Luddite comes to mind.

When it comes to playing, I haven't opened half the software games I've purchased because I don't have a week or so to figure the instructions. What really ticks me off is that by the time I make time to learn them, the price to purchase them has halved. And every time there is a power outage I cringe at the idea that I have to reprogram all the electrical gadgets I can no longer live without. What we really had to fear with the Y2K panic was that somehow all the electrical dog fences that are buried in people's lawns would fail and all the dogs in the world would run loose wreaking havoc in their neighborhoods.

So change is real. Our fear of change is real. And it is happening at an exponential rate. And that's the good news. So you can either move out West, shave your head, put on a home spun rob and join a commune, and forget about change or just deal with it.

I don't much care for home spun robes, they're breezy and I like what little bit of hair I still have, so I opt to deal with change. And yes, I still cringe and I still feel quizzy in my stomach every time I have to deal with change, however; what a great time this is to be alive. I can just imagine my kids telling their kids that not only did they have to walk to school and back home up hill both ways, they only had four television sets and they had to share a computer that could only access the World Wide Web. Oh the suffering!

THE ONE CONSTANT

Change is inevitable. I have seen unprecedented levels of change in almost every aspect of my life. I have come to the realization that the change process is speeding up rather than slowing down. I also realize that what I am experiencing is not unique but commonplace.

As managers we need to become the positive icon that shows others that we are committed to the changes that are necessary in order for our organizations to progress. It is only through change that true progress will take place.

There seems to be one constant today that we can all depend upon. That constant is *change*. We are living in a time where we are experiencing unprecedented change. We experience it at work and at home. We see and hear about it in the newspaper, magazines, television, and the Internet.

How we deal with change is as important as the change itself. I'm convinced one of the core competencies managers need to have now and into the 21st Century is the ability to deal with organizational change. In particular, every manager will need to understand and deal with the people aspect of change.

To do this we must understand that everyone will not embrace change. In fact, the following words by Robert Kennedy are more in line with what we can expect when attempting to progress by implementing change:

> *"Progress is a nice word. But change is its motivator and change has its enemies."*

So as managers, how do we implement change without creating unwanted enemies? To answer that question I have to say that there are many things in this world that we have little control over. But there is one thing we do have control over. We have control over our attitude as it relates to change. We can have an unenthusiastic outlook that reeks of negativism and pessimism. Woody Allen captured this sentiment quite well by saying:

> *"More than anytime in history mankind faces a crossroads. One path leads to despair and utter hopelessness, the other to total extinction. Let us pray that we have the wisdom to choose correctly."*

I prefer a more enlightened view of change. Choosing deliberately to be positive, optimistic, and enthusiastic towards change is the role of today's manager. By taking this type of attitude you can throw your energy into correcting problems rather than creating them.

Every manager must take some ownership of the changes that occur in the workplace. Personal responsibility for managing change needs to be part of every manager's job. To take that responsibility means that we need to be prepared to deal with and handle changes as they occur. Some of the things we should consider to prepare for and deal with change include the following:

Communicate - Stay informed on what is going on in your business and keep your people informed as well. If people don't know what is going on they can't be a part of the solution.

Heart - Management from the heart is the only way to manage in today's dynamic workplace. People won't care how much you know until they know how much you care.

Adapt - You need to be quick on your feet to keep up with all the changes that come your way. Embrace change as a natural process rather than something to be resisted at all costs. *"In a fight between you and the world, bet on the world." Franz Kafka*

Negativity - Your job as a manager is to eradicate negativity in the workplace by embracing an attitude of optimism and enthusiasm.

Grow - To deal with change you need to grow and you need to help your people grow. Make your organization a learning organization. *"Only those who constantly retool themselves stand a chance of staying employed in the years ahead." Tom Peters*

Exercise - Change can be very stressful. Exercise will make you feel better both physically and mentally. Physical activity offers release from tension at home and work.

Change is not an option, it is a constant. If you are committed to change you stand a far better chance of inspiring the commitment of others. So get out there and help invent the future. The progress of our organizations depends upon it.

PLANNING FOR CHANGE

Every organization is in a continuous state of change. When dealing with continuous change we have two options. The first option is to let change happen to you. The second option is to plan for change.

I prefer to plan for change. It cuts down on surprises. Not that anything is wrong with surprises. I think they are great when it's your birthday, other than that, surprises are something I'd just as soon avoid.

According to authors Harold Koontz & Cyril O'Donnell:

"Planning is deciding in advance what to do, how to do it, when to do it, and who is to do it. Planning bridges the gap from where we are to where we want to go. Planning makes it possible for things to occur which would not otherwise happen."

If we are to look at planning as a process, we would begin the process by asking ourselves four questions. These questions include:

- Where are we now?
- Where do we wish to go?
- What are the different ways of getting there?
- How will we know when we are there?

I've asked myself these questions each time I've taken on a new project. It seems no matter how large or how small the project is, these questions have a validity which makes all the difference between success and failure.

If you ask yourself these four basic questions, you have given yourself a powerful tool for achieving your objectives. Keep in mind that planning is not an end in itself, but it should precede all other management functions.

When asking yourself where you are now, you should do a quick scan of the environment. Observe what is going on and ask questions. Although we tend to depend on our instincts, we shouldn't lose sight of all the other sources of information we have available to us. These sources can be people, publications, studies, or other forms of valuable data.

Determining where you wish to go should be thoroughly researched. Unless you are the only one involved in planning for change, I suggest you get input from across the organization to make sure your compass is pointing in the right direction. Making decisions based upon poor or misconceived information can be disastrous and irreversible.

In determining the different ways to get to your planning objectives you should surround yourself with a diverse group of people. Planning should be a shared responsibility. By that I mean that our surest guarantee of successfully dealing with change and growth is to include as many talented people as feasible in the planning process. The diversity of other's is the key to generating ideas and tapping into human talent that will infuse new life into any project.

We also need to remember that once we've accomplished our objective it is time to move on to other challenges. As I said earlier, change is constant and so is the opportunity that accompanies it. When one project ends, another one is certain to take its place.

Whether you are dealing with changes at home or at work, your key to success is asking yourself some simple questions and then tapping into the people that have the talent to get things done. If you can tap into the potential of others you will drastically increasing the likelihood of your success. You will also decrease the chances that you will have to do everything yourself.

INNOVATION

"Organizational survival demands innovation which means perpetual creative destruction."

—Peter Drucker

"I've spent a good part of my life studying economic successes and failures… above all; I've learned that everything takes a back seat to innovation."

—Tom Peters

Innovation was not created in this century. Our history is replete with examples of how innovation literally changed the world. By expanding the length of their spears, Alexander and his strategy of using the Macedonian phalanx allowed him to conquer the known world. The Roman legions did the same thing by adding a small piece of lead to their pilums (spears) that would allow the spear point to bend once it struck the enemies shield, making it nearly impossible to remove the pilum and thus encumber the enemy.

To be effectively innovative we have to be leaders of change. Just like the Macedonian that got the idea to add a foot or two onto the length of their spears or the Roman that thought spears that bend would be a great idea. Can you imagine the Roman Tribune that was first approached with the idea? "Well sir, I think it would be a great idea if we changed our pilums so that when we throw them at someone, and they hit a shield, they will bend." I'd hate to have been in his sandals.

Today we are overwhelmed with stories of how a couple of people, down on their luck, spent their last $200.00 on some lame brained idea that no one else believed in. Yet, while working out of some drafty garage, they started a business that now employs thousands of people and is worth billions of dollars. To add insult to injury, we now realize that we could never live without whatever it was they invested their time, money, and energy on. Just take a look at a picture of Bill Gates and the group that started Microsoft. They didn't look like they could have scraped up a good idea or $200.00 amongst the entire group.

William Hewett and David Packard definitely fall into the "two guys and a garage" category. The only real difference is that they had $500.00 and no products to boast of. Instead, they entered into their business strategy with the simple idea that they would come up with new ways to use technology. Their strategy obviously worked, by 1996, their company was worth over 20 billion dollars.

Matthew J. Kiernan (1996) in his book *The Eleven Commandments of 21ˢᵗ Century Management,* feels strongly enough about the importance of innovation to include it as one of his commandments. According to Kiernen we have to get innovative or get dead. One way to do this is to include innovation in our strategic planning. If we do not intend to become innovative, chances are we won't be. Kiernen warns against a "steady as she goes" mentality within today's business environment. Who wants to be the captain of a doomed vessel? Constant innovation is needed just to survive.

Kiernen goes on to say that innovations in technology, production, marketing and finance are essential, but it is innovation in management and strategy that is most desperately in short supply. He also says that what separates truly great corporate innovators from the competitors they leave in the dust is their ability to create conscious mechanisms to innovate consistently.

Kiernen cites Canada's Syncrude as a company that learned how to leverage Native talent into an organizational asset. Syncrude is the world's largest producer of synthetic crude oil. The synthetic crude oil is extracted from oil and tar sands. This is a costly, difficult, and time-consuming operation.

Due in part to the remoteness of their operation near their largest crude oil deposit, Natives are hired to meet the demanding workload. Traditionally, Canada's Native people are not always seen as a sound human resource investment. Syncrude however, recognized the Native population as a viable human resource that could be used to meet the demands of their operation.

As is often the case, Syncrude went about training the Native people to fit in with their corporate culture. What they discovered was that the Native people had as much to offer Syncrude as Syncrude had to offer them. In particular, these indigenous people not only understood the concepts of teamwork, they actually practiced them. Teamwork was intrinsic to the Native team at Syncrude.

Syncrude discovered that it was good business to hire Native people. Their diversity allowed them to bring about a variety of innovations that helped bring about new and creative ideas at work. Some of these were in the area of business management and strategy, the very area that Kiernen insists is noticeably missing from many businesses today.

Illuminated leaders understand that innovation is needed if organizations are to survive and prosper. Innovation must expand beyond product and process development to include the human side of business. Old management principles and practices need to be carefully evaluated and changed to meet the demands of the 21ˢᵗ century. We need an intentionally balanced approach to innovation that includes changes in the way we manage our greatest resource, our people.

CULTURE

> *"Never before in the history of business has the impact of organizational culture been more critical to the success of organizations and the effectiveness of individuals leading them. The pace of change is so rapid that agile cultures, driven by high-performance teams, have become a competitive imperative. The knowledge and skills required to lead 21ˢᵗ-century organizations have changed dramatically."*
>
> —Larry E. Senn & John R. Childress
> *The Secret of a Winning Culture: Building High-Performance Teams*

For many, an organizations culture is best defined as "the way we do things around here." In reality, organizational culture is made up of shared values, beliefs, behaviors, heroes and systems. Many organizations are long overdue for a much needed change.

Changing an organizations' culture can be one of the most difficult tasks any leader can address. Some of the barriers that leaders face are obvious, others are hidden. According to Senn and Childress, there are early behavioral signs that point to resistance of cultural change. These signs of resistance include:

- Reluctance to accept ideas from other organizations (the "not invented here" syndrome)
- Turf issues and power struggles
- Groups forming under the protection of a politically strong individual that distance themselves from the change process
- Senior management having other priorities that prevent sufficient personal involvement and visibility
- Lip service and "malicious obedience"
- The "observer-critic" syndrome in which all new ideas are challenged
- People and groups blaming one another
- Hierarchical rigid structure
- Bureaucracy and resistance to change

The authors go on to explain that a recent study of Fortune 1000 companies estimated that 20% of people's time in an organization is wasted on issues related to the corporate culture. People spend too much time playing the victim, blaming others, justifying poor performance, and complaining why things should be different. This type of behavior negatively impacts an organization and establishes culture barriers.

There are signs that tell when an organization is in need of a positive culture change. These signs include: turf issues and resistance to change; too much hierarchy and bureaucracy; the blame game will be alive and well and excuses will prevail throughout the workplace; there will be a lack of customer focus and a lack of bias for action; trust will be in short supply; openness will be virtually non-existent, and the lack of a can-do attitude will be evident.

There are many ways to tackle the challenge of changing an organizations culture. Straight-forward communication is a good first step. Communicate the values of the organization and ensure these values are being discussed, shared and exhibited on a continuous basis. As an example, if you really believe customer focus is important, ensure your actions as a leader give undeniable credence to that value. Do you reward and or punish based upon how customers are treated? Does your performance program weigh-in heavily on the side of customer focus or not?

One of the biggest factors that must be addressed in order to bring about positive culture change is the degree of openness and trust. If people cannot speak openly and frankly about their concerns, culture change will not be possible.

Senn and Childress suggest every organization fully understand and answer the following questions in order to bring about culture change:

- What external competitive or marketplace forces are impacting our business?
- What is our internal readiness for change?
- How deep are issues of mistrust?
- How aligned is the senior team?
- What is the level of teamwork between departments?
- What are the key cultural barriers to change?
- What cultural and organizational changes are needed to support new competitive strategies or performance improvements?

For leaders to effectively bring about culture change, they must become the role models for the cultural values they want exhibited in their organization. This can only happen through meaningful introspection and a realistic self-inspection by senior level management. What then follows is a commitment to a cultural change that doesn't reflect what an organization currently looks like, but rather what it should look like. The challenge is in moving the organization from the present into the future.

Studies show that culture change is possible when an active culture-change program is in place. The changes are not immediate; it typically takes two to three years to reshape a culture. I suggest immediate action, the benefits are worth the effort and the time will pass anyway, so you might as well address culture change issues NOW.

PERSONAL GROWTH

"But in the world of the twenty-first century, we will all need to learn and grow throughout our careers. One of the many problems in complacent organizations is that rigidity and conservatism make learning difficult."

—John P. Kotter
Leading Change

Dave Ulrich, a professor of business administration at the School of Business, University of Michigan, and a partner in the Global Consulting Alliance wrote an article in 1996, "Credibility x Capability" published in "The Leader of the Future". In this article he shares that the leaders of the future will be known

- Less for what they say and more for what they deliver
- Less by their title and position and more by their expertise and competence
- Less by what they control and more by what they shape
- Less by goals they set and more by mind-sets they build
- Both for great personal credibility and for exceptional organizational capabilities

Kotter (1996) found the importance of lifelong learning in an increasing changing business environment and its relationship to leadership was demonstrated rather dramatically in a twenty-year study of 115 students from the Harvard Business School class of 1974. In attempting to explain why most were doing well in their careers despite the challenging economic climate that took shape at about the time they graduated, he found that two elements stood out: competitive drive and lifelong learning.

He determined the following mental habits supported lifelong learning:

- Risk taking – Willingness to push oneself out of comfort zones
- Humble self-reflection – Honest assessment of successes and failures, especially the latter
- Solicitation of opinions – Aggressive collection of information and ideas from others
- Careful listening Propensity to listen to others
- Openness to new ideas – Willingness to view life with an open mind

I learned a great deal about the importance of personal growth when I attended my daughters first science fair. I was a nervous parent who hoped my daughters efforts would be noticed by the judges and that her recycling project would be selected to go on to the state finals. It didn't, but I was proud of her effort. When she was one of the finalists to go on to the county competition I was still a nervous parent and I was also asked to be a judge. This time around the parents were watching as I interviewed a half-dozen kids about their projects.

I knowingly (while not knowing) nodded my head as a 13 year old explained that he had created a device to determine whether vibrations alter sound patterns. He showed me a device that was made up of a flashlight, oatmeal container, rubber bands, masking tape, and other household appliances. By the time I had interviewed and evaluated all six of the young boys and girls on my list it was totally evident. The nerds had won! And all I could think was that these kids had brighter futures than the ones that hadn't tried out for the science fair. They were imaginative, bright, and yes, many of them would be classified as nerds.

As an unenlightened youth I would have identified these gifted students using some of the following criteria: They were the ones that ran the school projection systems (when we still used 16mm film). They were the ones that always got the 4.0 average with what seemed to me to be very little effort. They were often in the marching band, student council, or were in the Scouts or 4H until they were kicked out due to age discrimination. Pocket protectors were not a luxury, they were a necessity. Basically we're talking about a parent's dream-come-true.

As a judge at the science fair I found the projects they had worked on were very creative. The findings were well documented. They were using the scientific method as though they were in a master's degree program rather than being in 7th and 8th grade. My wife and I both selected several of the young men as possible future mates for our daughter. To put it mildly, she didn't share our enthusiasm.

We all have a little bit of nerd in us. In fact, it is a good thing. I was never a 4.0 anything. I didn't really get interested in personal growth until I entered the work force and determined that education and knowledge were directly linked to take-home-pay. If I could take back the years and re-do them, I'd have considered pushing around the squeaky audiovisual cart, playing in the marching band, running for student council, wearing a pocket protector, and entering projects in the science fair. Maybe some of the nerdiness (this is a good thing) would have rubbed off.

The effective leader understands the importance of personal growth. They consistently ask, learn, follow-up and grow. Leaders who refuse to learn and grow will soon become ineffective and obsolete. Amazing what you can learn from a group of kids at a middle-school science fair.

RESILIENCY

The term "career resiliency" comes from an article written for the Harvard Business Review in 1994. The article was titled "Toward a Career-Resilient Workforce." The premise behind the article was that both the employee and employer share responsibility for maintaining and even enhancing an individual's employability.

Career self-reliance is the ability to actively manage your work and your life in a rapidly changing environment. It has to do with having an attitude of being self-employed whether you are inside or outside the organization.

Dr. Tom Peters addressed the issue of resiliency in his Fast Company article "Brand You." He stressed the need to continually learn, to grow, to improve your skills in order to become a more marketable asset. He expounded on the importance of training in order to become a resilient person.

Apparently, Dr. Peters and General Robert E. Lee shared a common understanding of the importance of training and education. General Lee said, "The education of a person is never completed until they die." I found his statement interesting, particularly given the time in which he lived (1807-1870). Peter Drucker explains:

> *"Throughout history, craftspeople who had learned a trade had acquired everything they would ever need to know during their lifetime after five or six years of apprenticeship. In Post-Capitalist Society, it is safe to assume that anyone with any knowledge will have to acquire new knowledge every four or five years, or else become obsolete."*

Drucker's comments help clarify the importance of career self-reliance. His advice should weigh heavily on our minds. It is the need for knowledge and for creativity that has made the concept of learning organizations a necessity for survival.

Organizations around the world find themselves in the midst of unprecedented change. We have only recently made the transition into the information age and are already moving beyond that into an age of global realignment. Yet many of our organizations are still modeled after successful industrial-era businesses.

For those individuals that are not pursuing training and education to improve themselves or their organizations it has been suggested that they ought not be allowed to wander around where they can do some serious damage. Ouch! These are tough words for challenging times. Unfortunately, by standing still we lose ground in the society portrayed by Drucker. That is why it is every person's responsibility to determine whether they want to be self-reliant, or to be found wandering around aimlessly.

Do yourself and your organization a big favor. Read a book, take a course, start a degree, finish a degree, learn to operate new software…There are a million ways to make ourselves more resilient, but every one of them begins with YOU.

THE LEADER AS GARDENER

"Please bear in mind one terribly important point that all gardeners, including experts, tend to forget. Each person is allotted a certain number of springs in his or her lifetime, and the number is considerably smaller than a cautious person would require to become an accomplished and successful gardener. To make the best use of this limited time, it is necessary to be bold, to take risks, to make mistakes, to experience disappointment and occasionally to waste money on bad ideas…Plants are living things and will behave in unexpected ways ranging from extravagant success to nearly instantaneous mortality. The more of them you have, the more surprises you will get, and it will eventually dawn on you, as it has on us, that it is the process, not the product, that is so extraordinarily satisfying."

—Amos Pettingill
White Flower Farm

I can't claim to be much of a gardener. I do look forward to spring each year as I see the flowers come into bloom. There is something special about the rejuvenation that takes place in the spring after a long cold winter. I can't take much credit for the flowers that grow in my yard but I do enjoy them.

I basically do the heavy lifting at home when it comes to gardening. My wife will work for hours in our flower gardens. I dig the holes and haul the water when I'm asked. It is my wife's vision and gardening abilities that gives us both so many hours of enjoyment. The outdoor work itself is refreshing and the outcome is inspiring.

As long as I can remember I've searched for and found abstract connections between events and lessons that can be learned about leadership. Gardening is no exception. Leaders and gardeners have much in common.

When I read the statement about gardens by Amos Pettingill I realized gardeners and leaders have a great deal in common. The gardener tends to the garden while the leader tends to the workplace. The workplace is the leader's garden where they hone their craft. The leader is to the gardener as the follower is to the flower.

The leader, like a gardener, is the visionary who creates the garden. They imagine, design and layout the garden to meet their needs. The gardener arranges the seeds and plants them in such a way as to bring about the effect they want while ensuring the arrangement is harmonious to their intent.

The leader, just like the gardener, must be a patient person because the results of their labor take time to manifest. They know that planting takes time and effort before seeing the fruits of their labor. The gardener and leader must be ever vigilant. Gardeners carefully plant seeds to ensure the seeds receive sunlight, water and nutrients; leaders must also take the time to thoughtfully place workers in the right place and in the right environment to nourish them and ensure their growth.

The gardener also understands the value of diversity. Flowers are diverse; they come in all sizes, shapes, colors, and textures. Some flowers are early bloomers; some are late bloomers while some bloom continuously. Some need very little attention while others need constant attention. Some followers might accurately be named after flowers such as the "Morning Glory" while others would receive names less desirable. Followers, like flowers are also unique and they grow and develop at their own pace. Some need more attention than others and every follower is unique. The best gardens, just like the best workplaces embrace diversity.

Some plants are aggressive and take over more space than allotted in the garden design so the gardener must keep them in check. Sometimes, the leader has followers that are aggressive and wrongfully assert themselves on others. The leader must deal with encroachment issues. Just like the flower, the follower must also have ample room to stretch and grow. This is how the follower learns new skills and makes mistakes without fear of reprisal. The workplace should be a safe haven for growth and development.

The gardener keeps their garden healthy and looking its best. They avoid disease and infestations by carefully observing plants, removing spent blossoms, performing maintenance, fertilizing, mulching, watering, inspecting for pests, division, staking, and other forms of gardening care.

The leader does the same types of things. They remove fear, dissension, apathy and other disorders and nuisances that contaminate or would otherwise harm the workplace. Great leaders observe their followers and tend to their needs.

Just like the gardener, it takes time to become an accomplished leader. Leaders must use the limited time they have wisely. They must be bold, take risks, make mistakes and experience joy and disappointments along the way. Exceptional leaders also know when to leave well enough alone.

People, like plants, are living things that will behave in unexpected ways and the more of them you lead the more surprises you will experience. Eventually it will dawn on you that it was the relationship with followers, not the end product that provided the greatest satisfaction.

SELF

"Why do we lose the sense that we are entitled to joy for its own sake? What happens to our willingness to ask others to help meet our needs? When do we start to feel guilty about pursuing pleasure and play? At what stage of development do we adopt the belief that our larger purpose is to serve everyone else's needs?"

—Alice D. Domar & Henry Dreher
*Self-Nurture: Learning to Care for Yourself as
Effectively as You Care for Everyone Else*

This may sound strange, particularly when we place so much emphasis on serving the needs of others. However, questions like these give us pause in order to reflect upon our relationship with self. We are so busy doing for others; we typically neglect our own needs. How sad is that? Domar and Dreher believe it is okay to grant our self the same tenderness and fierce protectiveness we'd otherwise reserve for a beloved child. "Self-nurture is not about being selfish. Its about self-care."

It is okay to allow yourself time for relaxation and pleasure. It is okay to allow yourself time for creative play. If we do not allow ourselves time to relax and to enjoy the good things that life has to offer, we become bitter and resentful. Typically, we madly rush around making sure everyone else's needs are met while we slowly but surely travel down the road to emotional and physical exhaustion.

How can we give to others when we are unwilling to give to self? Is it any wonder that stress has reached epidemic proportions? We are pulled between our work and a variety of other commitments. What time is left for self-nurturance when all of our time is spent in doing for others? Nurturance of the mind, body, and spirit is essential to our well being; yet thirty minutes of peace and quiet are often seen as a selfish and undeserved luxury.

Our models of self-nurturance were learned in childhood. What did we learn? Did we learn the importance of self-care or just the need to sacrifice for others? Maybe we were taught to doubt ourselves, to neglect our needs or even something much worse? Whatever the lesson, if we didn't learn the importance of self-nurture, it isn't too late. The deeper truth as explained by Domar and Dreher is that we can't please everyone if we ever hope to please ourselves.

We all need time for solitude and reflection. We must actively pursue our own personal interests in order to be interesting to others. If we do not have a relationship with self, the likelihood of a meaningful and fulfilling relationship with others is diminished.

Creative and relaxing pursuits should be at the top of our "to-do" list. Yet, these pursuits are often pushed to the bottom of the list because they are labeled as unimportant or unproductive. Anyone who has spent meaningful time on creative or relaxing pursuits can attest to the positive emotional hit they experienced. Our priorities should reflect the importance of self-nurturing pursuits.

As we age, for some unknown reason, we view activities that feel like play as unnecessary, even foolish. When did playground time become wasted time? Playground time becomes even more important to our physical, mental, and spiritual health as we age. According to Domar and Dreher:

> *"Play is at the heart of both creative expression and creative leisure. We do ourselves a favor when we recover the spirit of play, not just while on vacation but in our everyday activities, in solitude and relationship in productive work or totally unproductive recreation."*

Self-nurture allows for the nurturing of others. Self-deprivation…well I'm sure you get the picture. So take that trip you've been putting off. Go rent that movie you have wanted to see. Attend that seminar, visit that friend, play that game, or treat yourself to a long overdue visit to the spa. Cut yourself a break, you deserve it, and everyone you nurture will also benefit. Take care of yourself, so you can take better care of others.

SELFING

> *"Selfing means doing for one's Self, in the larger sense of Self, as in True Self, or "To thine own self be true." It means fulfilling the dreams, goals and aspirations inherent within us. It means living our life "on purpose."*
>
> —John-Roger & Peter McWilliams
> *Do It! Let's Get Off Our But*

According to John-Roger and McWilliams, Selfing is about knowing what we want for our self rather than looking to others for that answer. Being you and knowing what you want isn't being selfish, it is about personal awareness. Personal awareness allows each of us to live up to our possibilities rather than handing our individuality over to others. Moving toward self-awareness develops our unique character.

George Bernard Shaw captured the concept of selfing when he wrote:

> *"This is the true joy in life, the being used for a purpose recognized by yourself as a mighty one; the being thoroughly worn out before you are thrown on a scrap heap; the being a force of nature instead of a feverish selfish little clod of ailments and grievances complaining that the world will not devote itself to make you happy."*

Because we live in a finite world, we must make purposeful decisions that lead us on our own unique path of accomplishment. There are four basic areas we live in. These areas include our family life, professional life, social life, and spiritual life. How we spend our time and energy in these areas should be reflective of our purpose in life.

The key word here is "should." When we spend an equal amount of time in each category we are considered to have a balanced life. Balance is good, yet a balanced life does not generally allow a person to reach the heights of accomplishment they are capable of in any of the four categories.

Mother Theresa spent a lot of time on spiritual development. Donald Trump did the same thing with his professional life. When we spend most of our time in just one category we are likely to be imbalanced in other categories. Personal choices should be made with some level of planned awareness and an understanding that happiness is more likely when our lives are balanced and we meet or exceed our personal expectations.

Henry Wadsworth Longfellow explained:

> "The heights by great men reached and kept were not attained by sudden flight, but they, while their companions slept, were toiling in the night."

Effective selfing is about narrowly defining our personal goals so that we can effectively and efficiently manage our time, energy and resources. Balancing family, professional, social, and spiritual life is no easy task. Making time for yourself and ensuring your unique talents are developed and nurtured can sometimes seem impossible. Selfing is needed if we are going to fulfill our dreams, goals, and aspirations.

Is that being selfish? No, it is about being yourself and bringing your best self into the world. We all have special gifts, unfortunately; we sometimes forget who we are and what we are suppose to be doing. Our time is often spent on some unproductive tangent that keeps us from our true purpose in life.

We must evaluate who we are and whether we are on the right path. Being on the right path is the ultimate goal and the path is littered with obstacles. Friends, although well meaning, are often accomplices in our misplaced sense of purpose. When you know your purpose in life, look for those who can assist you in reaching your goals.

We often forget that the most important relationship is our relationship with self and that our relationship with others is a choice. Your relationship with self will go on your entire life. Take care of yourself and make sure you are on the right path, whatever that path might be. Remember that being you and knowing what you want and then going for it isn't selfish, it is the manifestation of personal awareness.

Action plan for personal transformation:

- Create your own inspirational vision.
- Take initiatives that show your unique brilliance.
- Step forward and make a difference.
- Find new ways to enhance personal and organizational performance.
- Choose deliberately to be positive, optimistic and enthusiastic towards change.
- Surround yourself with talented and diverse people.
- Innovate or die.
- Bring about a positive culture change through openness and trust.
- Consistently and efficiently ask, learn, follow-up, and grow.
- Take care of yourself in order to fulfill your dreams, goals and aspirations.

Reflective Thoughts

3
Communication

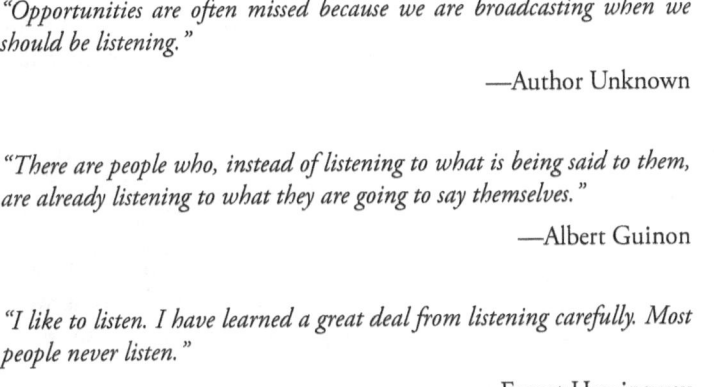

"Opportunities are often missed because we are broadcasting when we should be listening."

—Author Unknown

"There are people who, instead of listening to what is being said to them, are already listening to what they are going to say themselves."

—Albert Guinon

"I like to listen. I have learned a great deal from listening carefully. Most people never listen."

—Ernest Hemingway

The illuminated leader is someone who understands how to communicate. Effective communication is a behavior that is more important than ever. It is amazing that so little time is spend in learning the art of communication and in particular the art of listening when it has such an impact on both personal and organizational success.

The traits associated with communication are many and unfortunately under-utilized. One of the most effective attributes of a great communicator is their willingness to *smile* at others. A smile can open doors and break down barriers with relative ease. Have you ever walked into a meeting with a bunch of sour-pusses? Fun wasn't it! A simple smile sends the message that you are ready, willing, and able to communicate with the other person. It tells others that you are approachable, reduces fear, and sets the stage for success.

The illuminated leader understands the importance of *listening*. They typically spend more time, considerably more time listening than talking. Have you ever spent time with someone who spent more time talking than listening? The word "irritating" comes to mind. Great communicators listen intently to both the words and emotions of others. They suspend their judgment and invest themselves completely in what the other person has to say.

The really great communicators understand their audience. The late President Ronald Reagan was known as "The Great Communicator" because he understood his audience. He didn't talk down to people; he used language that everyone could understand.

There are those we might classify as *smart-talkers*. Beware of them. Illuminated leaders can spot smart-talkers a mile away. Smart-talkers are more about the words they use than the content of the message they send. Their communication style is designed to impress rather than enlighten. The smart-talkers communication is geared toward self-advancement no matter the consequences. Their words lack substance and are backed only with self-promotion and an unhealthy dose of ego.

Great communication has substance and is intended to enlighten. The illuminated leader speaks from the *heart*. There is great power in an emotional message that others resonate with.

Speaking the *truth* greatly simplifies every form of communication. The illuminated leader always speaks the truth. Through truth telling we gain the trust of others. Trust is too precious a commodity to ever lose. Illuminated leaders always tell the truth.

To be effective at communication we must remember that everyone is entitled to their opinion. Be patient with others as they express themselves. If we are uncertain of someone's meaning it is most appropriate to emulate Socrates by asking pertinent questions that eventually bring us to the point of understanding.

Communications can be tough and misunderstanding is often the norm, yet; one of the most critical behaviors a leader must learn and practice is how to effectively communicate.

DIALOGUE

"The most important work in the new economy is creating conversations."

—Alan Webber, editor
Fast Company magazine

"Dialogue is both rooted deeply in our ancestral past--helping us remember the sacredness and value of relationship--as well as being aligned with

twenty-first century thinking, it can be seen as the bridge between where we are now and where we want to go."

—Linda Ellinor & Glenna Gerard
Dialogue

The roots of the word *dialogue* come from the Greek words *dia* and *logos*. *Dia* means "through"; *logos* translates to "word," or "meaning." In essence, a dialogue is a *flow of meaning*. But it is more than this too. In the most ancient meaning of the word, *logos* meant "to gather together," and suggested an intimate awareness of the relationships among things in the natural world. In that sense, *logos* may be best rendered in English as "relationship."

Traditionally, we can trace dialogue the talking circles of American Indians, to the marketplace of ancient Greece, and to the tribal customs of indigenous people from all around the world. In dialogue we see the whole among the many parts, the connections between parts. We make inquiry into assumptions and learn from that inquiry. When we dialogue we create a shared meaning.

Dialogue is vastly different than discussion or debate. In discussion and debate we tend to break issues into parts, to see distinction between the parts. We tend to justify ourselves by defending our assumptions. We also persuade by selling or telling only our story. We see agreement as having only one meaning and that meaning is our meaning.

Some other defining qualities of dialogue are shared by Ellinor and Gerard and include:

- Suspension of judgment
- Release of the need for specific outcomes
- An inquiry into and an examination of underlying assumptions
- Authenticity
- A slower pace with silence between speakers
- Listening deeply to self, others, and for collective meaning

The concept of dialogue was expertly practiced by American Indians. In American Indian council meetings, a talking stick was passed to signify who had the floor. It prevented cross talk from occurring, honored the words spoken and showed respect for the person holding it.

According to the Iroquois constitution, the Iroquois (Onondaga) opened each council meeting by greeting one another and expressing gratitude by offering thanks to the earth where all people lived. Their gratitude extended to nature and all of its bounty. Their gratitude also extended to the Great Spirit, the wind, the skies above and even to the moon. This was all done before the council could begin.

Deborah Tannen, Ph.D., addresses many aspects of communication between women and men in her book *Talking From 9 to 5*. Her studies show that women and men do communicate differently. She points out that our culture is sometimes unkind to those that cross the invisible border that separates gender based communication.

According to Tannen, some of the conversational rituals that are most common among men involve using opposition such as banter, joking, teasing, and playful put-downs, and expending effort to avoid the one-down position in the interaction. Conversational rituals common among women are often ways of maintaining an appearance of equality, taking into account the effect of the exchange on the other person, and expending effort to downplay the speakers' authority so they can get the job done without flexing their muscles in an obvious way. Tannen explains:

> *"Men whose oppositional strategies are interpreted literally may be seen as hostile when they are not, and their efforts to ensure that they avoid appearing one-down may be taken as arrogance. When women use conversational strategies designed to avoid appearing boastful and to take the other person's feelings into account, they may be seen as less confident and competent than they really are."*

This could very well explain why so many men refuse to ask for directions, even when they are hopelessly lost. It seems no matter how many times we go to Cincinnati (when I'm driving); we always end up in Kentucky somehow. Kentucky is a great state, but that was not my destination. The real hard part here is making it seem like I really wanted to go to Kentucky in the first place.

It is the job of every leader to understand how to dialogue and know the differences in gender-based communication styles. Understanding individual styles are key to making informed decisions. Just because someone seems absolutely sure about something doesn't mean they really have a clue as to what is going on. On the other hand, just because someone comes across as being less confident doesn't mean they are less confident. Men downplay their doubts while women downplay their certainty.

Tannen cites Anthropologist Marjorie Harness Goodwin who found that girls criticize other girls who stand out by talking in ways that display self-confidence. Sounding too sure of themselves made them unpopular with their peers. Therefore, social inhibition against seeming to boast can make women appear less confident than they really are.

Goodwin found that girls discover they get better results if they phrase their ideas as suggestions rather than orders, and if they give reasons for their suggestions in terms of the good of the group. But while these ways of talking make girls and, later, women—more likable, they make women seem less competent and self-assured in the world of work.

The rules for boys, as you might expect are a little different. Boys' tend to be hierarchical. One-upsmanship is the name of the game. Boys try to take center-stage more often than girls and they do this by telling jokes, stories and other ways to gain attention. They tend to work at staying in charge and often do this by giving orders. There actions can be interpreted as high levels of self-esteem and confidence

There are no hard and fast rules that apply to everyone, regardless of gender. Unfortunately, there are many people who feel we should all fulfill their expectations of how men and women should communicate. In their minds, men that are not very aggressive or women that are too aggressive just don't compute. The difference between being seen as a go-getter or as being arrogant is a matter of degree, and the formula is different for every single observer. Being aware of this dynamic allows us to relate more effectively with others.

The real key to effective communication is to use dialogue as our default. We could learn a lot about communicating from the talking circles of the American Indian councils of the past.

LISTENING

"People do not listen, they reload."

—Anonymous

"Don't talk unless you can improve on the silence."

—Laurence C. Coughlin

"Dialogue is not just talking with one another. More than speaking, it is a special way of listening to one another--listening without resistance...it is listening from a stand of being willing to be influenced."

—Anonymous

We tend to prepare ourselves whenever we want or need to speak. What we seem to be lacking is the same amount of preparation when we need to listen. One way to prepare ourselves to listen is to be still. We need to quiet our inner voice, to do as our tribal ancestors did. They were attuned to their surroundings. Their language was deeply rooted in the physical sounds of the earth, the birds and the beasts, the flow of streams and rivers. We need to ask ourselves, what is our language deeply rooted to?

To really listen, you have to first be still. You have to look for the meaning in the words of others. To look for their reactions and the reactions you have to their words. It is only after listening that you can effectively speak your voice.

We tend to admire those that speak their mind and their heart. Yet, how can you speak your mind and your heart if you haven't taken the time to listen? Isaacs in Dialogue *and the Art of Thinking Together* explains:

> *"If I speak, it is often to make my point, to indicate my superiority to claim my ground. Often I lie in wait in meetings, like a hunter looking for his prey, ready to spring out at the first moment of silence. My gun is loaded with pre-established thoughts. I take aim and fire, the context irrelevant, my bullet and its release all that matter to me."*

Isaacs sees respect as one of the secrets to the dialogic way of being. There must be a willingness to forgive that which we see in another and come to the point where we can accept what we see in our self. He says this implies coming to a place of respect both for others and for us.

In the November 1998 issue of GQ magazine, Michael Kaplin wrote an article that addresses one aspect of communications that finds relevance in a very odd setting. This historically Swedish custom has relevance to today's business environment. Kaplin explains how Nils Yngve Bergqvist, an hotelier in the northern Swedish village of Jukkasjarvi, helped launch the Sauna Academy.

The academy was founded to promote the greater good of sauna. Some would say the real advantage is to give the locals a cozy retreat for drinking beer and conversing on subjects of interest. The real importance of sauna as a Swedish tradition is dialogue. According to Kaplin:

> *"Passing around a bottle of 160-proof Stroh 80, the doctor insists cleanliness and warmth were the initial attractions of the 500-year-old heat-bath tradition. It's how the (badly outnumbered) Finnish army beat up the Russians in many battles during World War II.'...It was a good way for the generals to meet with their men—you get undressed and everybody is equal. It's the same thing now...With the sweat comes instant kinship and the same conversational intimacy fostered by poker tables and fishing holes...In the sauna you speak truth."*

Here are some ideas you can use to more effectively listen to what others have to say:

- Take time to greet everyone.
- Smile.
- Meet in a circle if possible, it makes everyone equal. There was a reason King Arthur met at a round table.
- Make direct eye contact with everyone – scan the room so everyone feels included.

- Spend more time listening than talking
- Don't allow anyone to dominate meetings.
- Suspend judgment.
- Ask questions instead of giving answers. That is what Socrates would have done.

DEEP LISTENING

"I believe we can change the world if we start listening to one another again. Simple, honest, human conversation. Not mediation, negotiation, problem-solving, debate, or public meetings. Simple, truthful conversation where we each have a chance to speak, we each feel heard, and we each listen well."

—Margaret J. Wheatley
Turning to One Another

According to consultant and professional speaker Margaret Wheatley, "Human conversation is the most ancient and easiest way to cultivate the conditions for change—personal change, community and organizational change, planetary change." She understands how important it is to sit together and talk about the things that are important in our lives. But how often do we take the time to talk to others about all those issues that come into play as we move along the path we call life? How often do we listen to those who need to share their concerns and feelings? A quick glance at local and worldwide news gives us the true answer to these questions. Not often enough.

While visiting ancient Pueblo cliff dwellings in Colorado I noticed that kivas were an integral part of every community. The large number of kivas found at various archeological sites helps explain the importance placed on beliefs, ceremony and conversation amongst early American Indian culture.

The kivas were mostly underground, circular in shape, and included space for an altar and fireplace. Kivas had a hole in the roof that allowed people to enter and leave while letting in sunlight. Each kiva had a sipapu (hole in the floor) that symbolized the place where the mythical tribal ancestors first emerged from the primordial underworld regions into the earthly realm.

Upon entering a kiva I realized the Anasazi, which are believed to be the forbearers of the present day Pueblo culture, understood the importance of conversation. In modern Pueblos, groups of men and women form special societies to care for the spiritual needs of the village. According to the Mesa Verde Museum, these societies had several major concerns: ensuring favorable growing weather, curing illness, guaranteeing successful hunts and harvests, bringing about village harmony and perpetuation of the people.

When ceremonies weren't taking place, the kiva was used as a work area or as a social gathering place. This was a gathering place where great importance was placed on the need to honestly share ones thoughts and concerns. I imagined dialogues concerning weather, food, celebration, and relationships.

The kiva is the ancient version of the modern day conference room (or Starbucks for some). The circular kivas encouraged eye contact and true 360-degree feedback. Today, tables are generally square or rectangular. Eye contact is difficult at best. Without eye contact, conversations can't take place. Further, unlike the kivas of old, modern meeting rooms lack any sense of sacredness and seldom bring us to the point of sharing our true thoughts and concerns.

Efficient meetings are the hallmark of most organizations and relationship building isn't generally on the agenda. It takes time, real time to converse with others. It is through conversations that we build meaningful and long lasting relationships. Conversation is the path we must take to connect to others.

It is time to reawaken the practice of conversation and embrace it as an integral part of our lives. This ancient practice is needed. Our ancestors understood the value of conversation. Just as they wanted to be heard, we need to be heard. Just as they were willing to thoughtfully listen to others, we need to listen to others. Wheatley gives us some good reasons to converse:

> *"When we humans don't talk to one another, we stop acting intelligently. We give up the capacity to think about what's going on. We don't act to change anything. We become passive and allow others to tell us what to do. We forfeit our freedom. We become objects, not people. When we don't talk to each other, we give up our humanity."*

Robert Haskell, Ph.D., author of *Deep Listening: Hidden Meanings in Everday Conversation*, says "It's during coffee breaks and after meetings are over, when 'free-flowing' conversation is the rule, that many topics are thrown out for possible discussion."

Speaking the truth may be a risky business in environments where open and honest feedback is discouraged or punished. The closest some businesses will ever come to hearing the truth is in casual conversation outside the boardroom.

Unconscious meaning abounds in conversations but we often miss the hidden message others send. We must train ourselves to listen for key words, phrases, and the tone in people's voices to fully grasp the meaning of their message.

A good way to better understand what people are thinking is through informal conversations where we can randomly converse on a variety of topics. This provides an opportunity to observe both conscious and unconscious thoughts in a non-hostile environment.

Haskel emphasizes, "It's during times of informal chatter that unconscious meanings are most clearly visible." He goes on to say:

"Listening carefully beneath the words and stories of friends, family, and coworkers can reveal eternal human feelings and concerns of favoritism, rivalry, jealousy, competition, sexual feelings, gender issues, and leadership and authority concerns, as well as attitudes about racial and ethnic relationships."

If there is one skill that is invaluable in forming a long lasting and meaningful relationship, it is listening. We must be deep listeners. We must be sitting on the edge of our seat listeners. We must be hanging onto every word someone says listeners. We must be turning off the television and make eye contact with the other person listeners. And we must be smart listeners.

Always listen to what is said and interpret what is not said. The real message may be hidden in the unspoken word, the averted eye, the nervous twitch or clenched fist. Asking others what they really think when you are responsible for writing their performance appraisal doesn't lend itself to a totally truthful response. Leaders must seek truth by listening and looking for truth.

Deep listening is impacted by our past. Personal weaknesses, issues from 3rd grade or a miscommunication that happened a decade ago impacts understanding what someone says. Negative self-talk haunts nearly everyone. Is it any wonder people's willingness to communicate diminishes over time? Reticence is a learned habit that is self-justified due to the chronic inattentiveness of others and an unwillingness to believe in the good intentions of others.

We must continually ask ourselves whether we are truly listening to others. We must ask ourselves because listening is a sacred act. It is how we commune; enter into fellowship, association, participation, union and relationships.

Ponder for a few moments on when and with whom your most meaningful and fulfilling relationships have taken place. Was deep listening an important part of the formula for that successful relationship? Chances are it was. When a relationship ended in disaster, was nominal listening part of the formula for disaster? It probably was. So remember to take every opportunity to listen deeply to the intended words of others. Listen deeply for their good intentions. Do this at work, at home, and at play and maybe you will get it right some of the time.

LEARNING TO LISTEN

"Power lives more in listening than in talking. In fact, listening may be the key skill of the successful person. As soon as people feel that they've been listened to, they begin to evolve…People, especially when they have strong feelings are so caught up in their own point of view that they are listening for opposition. It completely disarms them when you refuse to play. There is

*an electric moment of possibility when you listen to another human being
with no agenda, no wanting them to see it your way. Pure listening."*

— Gay Hendricks, Ph.D., Kate Ludeman, Ph.D.
The Corporate Mystic

According to Hendricks and Ludeman, there are three phases of learning to listen.
The first phase is being able to summarize the content of what you've heard. This
sounds like an easy thing to do but this ability can take years to learn.

The authors write about a friend who learned to listen. He went with his
wife to a party where he knew almost no one. He decided not to try to impress
everyone, but rather to do nothing all evening but listen carefully and restate
what each person said to him. "On the way home his wife, glowing with
pride, she told him that several people had remarked about what a powerful,
charismatic, and articulate person he was." If power is our ability to influence
others, listening is the key.

The second stage of learning to listen is to resonate what the other person is
saying, particularly the emotional content. The authors call this "listening for
empathy." We need to resonate with the emotions of the speaker. We literally
imagine what it feels like for the person who is attempting to communicate.
Are they happy, sad, angry, or excited? Are their words in sync with their
emotions? What is the real message?

Dr. Tom Peters in his book *Re-Imagine: Business Excellence in a Disruptive
Age* validates the need for leaders to connect with others. Peters also tells an
intriguing story that is worth heeding:

> *"Ms. X had sat at dinner between Mr. Y and Mr. Z. Mssrs. Y and Z were
> renowned individuals. Z in particular. Said Ms. X about Mr. Y. "When you
> sat at dinner with him, you came away believing that he was perhaps the
> smartest individual you'd ever met." About Mr. Z (the truly successful one),
> she said, "When you sat at dinner with Mr. Z, you came away thinking that
> you were the smartest person on earth."*

To get this second stage of listening right requires an affinity for investing
in meaningful relationships. For relationships to really work, we must sincerely
desire to coalesce and be willing to invest the time needed.

The third stage of learning to listen comes when two people have done
enough of stages one and two to develop an alliance. With the goodwill
developed by stages one and two, they begin to listen to each other in a way
that sparks the creativity of each to heights they could not have reached on
their own. Hendricks and Ludeman concisely explain:

> *"This deep listening—listening to inspire mutual creativity—is responsible
> for many breakthroughs in the world. Listening for mutual creativity is rooted*

in two questions: What do you most want? And how can I help you get what you most want? To listen in total support of other people—to be for their goals and aspirations in your own body, mind, and spirit—may well be the greatest gift you can give your fellow human beings."

We must learn to listen. Those who are truly successful at developing relationships understand the power of listening. We must learn to listen to others without opposition. When you listen to another human being with no agenda, you are engaged in pure listening.

SMART-TALK

"The key to success in business is action. But in most companies people are rewarded for talking – and the longer, louder, and more confusingly, the better."

—Jeffrey Pfeffer & Robert Sutton
The Smart-Talk Trap

According to Pfeffer and Sutton, mission statements provide a familiar example of how executives allow talk to substitute for action. They studied several securities firms and investment banks. These organizations spent long hours crafting elegant mission statements that extolled the values of teamwork, integrity, and respect for the individual. But partners at those firms treated their young analysts like short-term contractors. They not only gave them work that wasn't commensurate with their skills but also were often openly impolite and even abusive.

When this behavior was mentioned to the leaders of one of the investment banks, they reacted with incredulity. Disrespectful behavior was precluded by their mission statement, they said-it couldn't be happening. The executives assumed that saying something made it so. Reality, however, proved that merely saying something guarantees nothing.

When it comes to mission statements, Eileen Shapiro suggests in her book, *Fad Surfing in the Boardroom*: they are little more than "a talisman, hung in public places, to ward off evil spirits." And sometimes, they don't even do that.

Pfeffer and Sutton contend that part of the smart-talk problem is the essence of management education at leading institutions in the United States and throughout the world. Students learn how to sound smart in classroom discussions and how to write smart things on essay examinations. A substantial part of students' grades is usually based on how much they say and how smart they sound in class.

Lets compare business education with the training people receive when their performance is a matter of life and death. Soldiers, pilots, and surgeons all receive classroom training, of course, but it quickly turns into learning by doing. The military requires soldiers to perform the very maneuvers that will be necessary during wartime. Pilots get into the cockpit and take off. In surgery, there is an old saying that describes how residents learn a procedure: "Hear one, see one, do one." In business education, the saying would go, "Hear one, talk about one, talk about one some more."

Their observations of contemporary organizations show that people who talk frequently are more likely to be judged by others as influential and important—considered leaders.

Numerous organizational and anthropological studies support the fact that some people talk more than others in order to come out on top. Research supports what Bernard Bass, in the classic summary of scholarly studies on leadership, Bass and Stogdill's *Handbook of Leadership*, has called the "babble" or "blabbermouth" theory of leadership:

> *"The theory states that people who talk more often and longer—regardless of the quality of their comments—are more likely to emerge as leaders of new groups, to be identified as leaders by observers of the group, to be viewed as influential by both group members and outsiders, and to have greater influence on group decisions."*

Pfeffer and Sutton explain that people who want to get ahead in organizations learn that talking a lot helps them reach their goal more reliably than taking action or inspiring others to act. And once people reach the heights, they are expected to talk more than ever. By dominating the groups' "airtime," they let everyone know who is in charge.

They go on to explain that it can be difficult to blame people for using smart-talk when it is used to do well in school or to move up the corporate ladder. But there is a more negative component of smart talk—the tendency to tear an idea down without offering anything positive in its place, and the belief that complex language and ideas are somehow better than simple ones.

They interestingly noted at a global financial institution, junior executives made a point—especially in meetings with their bosses present—of trashing the ideas of their peers. Every time someone dared to offer an idea, everyone around the table would leap in with reasons why it was nothing short of idiotic. Senior executives didn't try to stop the verbal fray. Sometimes they even nodded approvingly as smart-sounding fault finder's critiqued ideas to death.

The evidence that being critical of others makes a person appear smarter is not just anecdotal. Teresa Amabile, a professor at Harvard Business School, confirmed the point in a 1983 study called "Brilliant but Cruel." Amabile found that people who wrote negative book reviews were perceived by others as being less likable but more intelligent, competent, and expert than people who wrote positive reviews of the same books. She summarized her findings by noting; "Only pessimism sounds profound. Optimism sounds superficial."

Studies show that people will try to sound smart not only by being critical but also by using trendy, pretentious, or overblown language. Sometimes managers themselves don't know what they're talking about when they use complex language.

They are not claiming that complex language and concepts never add value to an organization. They are saying that they bring a lot less value than most executives realize. It was observed that the most common reaction to complexity was confusion.

In their estimation, the right kind of talk can inspire and guide intelligent action. It's just that talk can't be allowed to become a substitute for action. Fortunately, not all organizations are plagued by the knowing-doing gap. Some have managed to avoid the smart-talk trap. In those companies, people consistently say smart things, then do them. What typifies such organizations? Their research suggests that they share five characteristics:

- They have leaders who know and do the work.
- They have a bias for plain language and simple concepts.
- They frame questions by asking "how," not just "why."
- They have strong mechanisms that close the loop.
- They believe that experience is the best teacher.

The lesson here is that we need to keep our communications simple. If someone appears to be using smart-talk, then call them on it. Talk is cheap and action does speak louder than words. Communication works best when it is direct and easily understood. Benjamin Franklin had the right idea when he so aptly said, "A pair of good ears will drink dry a hundred tongues."

CONVERSATION

> *"Few practices seem to lie more at the heart of human communities than talking and telling the old stories. As far as I know, no indigenous culture has yet been found that does not have the practice of sitting in a circle and talking. Whether it is council circles, or women's circles, or circles of elders, it seems to be one of the truly universal practices among humankind. As commonly expressed in American Indian cultures, "You talk and talk until the talk starts."*

> —Peter Senge
> *The Fifth Discipline: The Art &*
> *Practice of the Learning Organization*

William Isaacs, *Dialogue and the Art of Thinking Together,* tells a story about Peter Senge who, after giving a speech, was asked to meet with twenty-five executives, mostly CEOs and executive VPs. Rather than present more, or conducting a question and answer session, he suggested that the group put their chairs in a circle and do a "check-in." According to Senge, this is one of the simplest practices of dialogue, going around the circle and saying a few words about whatever thoughts and feelings are moving in a person at the time.

I recently experienced this same type of conversation as part of a senior leadership meeting. We sat in a room and took the time to converse over accomplishments and issues that had taken place over the past year. After two hours of repeatedly going around the circle I sensed that everyone had spoken their mind. This simple practice was the most honest and open form of communication this group had practiced in nearly two years. This was a good investment of time. Everyone walked away knowing they had been given the opportunity to freely and openly express their feelings and concerns.

Dialogue can be defined as a form of shared inquiry, a way of thinking and reflecting together. It isn't something you do to another person. Dialogue is something you do with people. It is a form of inquiry that takes place between people. It is through dialogue that we tap into the collective consciousness. According to Isaacs:

> *"Too many of us have lost touch with the fire of conversation. When we talk together, it is rarely with depth. For the most part, we see our conversations as either opportunities to trade information or arenas in which to win points."*

Dialogue can be seen as communication with heart added into the equation. If you want to know what that feels like just take time to listen to the speeches of Dr. Martin Luther King Jr. His messages to the masses were heartfelt yet accurately expressed his deepest concerns in such a way that everyone, regardless of education or background could understand. His speeches made you feel like you were the only one in the audience and he was conversing directly with you. Some important lessons on how to effectively use conversation comes from the past and is shared with us by Isaacs:

> *"Wherever one looks throughout history, one can see evidence of tribal gatherings, community events, and councils, where the central glue of human organizing was conversation—often around a fire—usually carried on for days at a time. These rituals of conversation typically included everyone in a tribe. In South Africa, for example, indigenous people still hold gatherings where the eldest and the youngest are all treated with the same respect, where everyone is seen and recognized."*

Considerable power can be unleashed in dialogue. Unfortunately, we often fall back on argument and debate as a form of communication when the going gets tough. In business settings in particular, our language stems more from the "machine age" than from our ancient memories of dialogue. The ancient memories of dialogue still burn in us much like the tribal fires that burned brightly long, long, ago. These embers can be re-ignited, and in their re-ignition, we can tap into the power of people through their dialogue.

Isaacs points out that in Antarctica, recent studies of the survival habits of emperor penguins have brought some intriguing findings to light. It had been a mystery how these animals could survive the intense winds and frigid temperatures of this strange continent. Temperatures of fifty degrees below zero Fahrenheit and winds of one hundred miles an hour or more are not uncommon there. It turns out they survive by forming circles with their bodies nestled together, to retain heat. And then they slowly rotate the circle, so that no one bird is exposed to the wind too long.

Forming a circle is a metaphor for the power of dialogue. We can use dialogue as a way to deal with the challenges we face in all aspects of our lives. Forming a circle and using dialogue effectively, can help us survive. Here we have another lesson we can learn from observing our natural surroundings.

In 1995, the 104th Congress literally shut down the federal government over the 1995 budget battles with President Clinton. By late 1996, David Skaggs, a five-term Democratic congressman had had enough of the hostile debating and conflict that he labeled "the metaphysics of mistrust" among his fellow legislators. So he decided to do something about all the mistrust that was poisoning the political process.

In March of 1997, 215 members of the House attended a three-day retreat (without the media or staff members) in Hershey, Pennsylvania along with their spouses (who participated in the meetings) and their children. One of the most successful parts of the retreat was considered to be a train ride that allowed the legislators to see each other with their families in a non-adversarial role. The conversation tone that developed during the retreat would become known as the "Spirit of Hershey".

Amazing what we can accomplish just by practicing the art of conversation. Try it, you might like it and the results can be amazing.

TRUTH

> "We need our gadflies, whether we call them dissidents, whistle-blowers, mavericks, or even revolutionaries. Every organization, every society, rots from the top when it suppresses or ignores criticism. Healthy organizations as well as healthy societies thrive on what Socrates calls their freedom, their willingness to look at all the evidence in the search for truth. But this role of challenging the status quo cannot be left to others. Each of us must be a gadfly of sorts, from time to time, in our own way, in our community and organizations, if not on the national level."
>
> —Ronald Gross
> *Socrates Way: Seven Master Keys to Using Your Mind to the Utmost*

Ronald Gross uses the teachings of Socrates to explain the importance of telling the truth. According to Gross, Socrates' commitment to tell the truth had three aspects. They were personal, social, and political. Socrates felt the need to confront those who deluded themselves, social practices that needed scrutiny and political issues that were misunderstood. "As a result, Socrates has always been a mentor for men and women who have felt the need for honesty. The name of Socrates has been invoked from the jail cells of Thoreau, Gandhi, and Martin Luther King, Jr., each imprisoned for acts of civil disobedience."

In retrospect, we recognize the truth and the price some have paid. Socrates serves as an example of someone who spoke the truth regardless of the consequences. His willingness to endure the negative reactions of others made him an inspiring figure. Telling the truth when it is convenient isn't considered radical honesty. Gross cites a psychotherapist named Blanton who is based in Washington, D.C., who says, "Radical honesty is a kind of communication that is direct, complete, open, and expressive," he explains. "It's an authentic sharing of what you think and feel."

We are challenged sometimes by others to speak the truth. Being radically honest can make us very uncomfortable. We can begin by promising to speak the truth to ourselves. To speak the truth Blanton suggests we gather some good friends or colleagues and agree to experiment with telling the truth, including the truth about personal anger and resentment.

We should also commit ourselves to speaking the truth in our organization and our profession. When we think of certain professions, do we believe radical honesty or lying is the norm? Here is what Sissela Bok says in her book *Lying: Moral Choice in Public and Private Life*:

> *"Government officials and those who run for elections often deceive when they can get away with it and when they assume that the true state of affairs is beyond the comprehension of citizens. Social scientists condone deceptive experimentation on the ground that the knowledge gained will be worth having. Lawyers manipulate the truth in court on behalf of their clients. Those in selling, advertising, or any form of advocacy may mislead the public and their own competitors in order to achieve their goals. Psychiatrists may distort information about their former patients to preserve confidentiality or to keep them out of military service. And journalists, police investigators, and so-called intelligence operators often have little compunction in using falsehoods to gain the knowledge they seek."*

We should also speak the truth in our community, nation, and the world. Socrates spoke the truth in the Athens of his day. When Socrates walked the streets of Athens he could be heard by no more than 40,000 citizens. At the time, he didn't know his words would be influential 2,500 years later. One person can have a powerful impact that can stand the test of time.

AGONISM

> *"Our spirits are corroded by living in an atmosphere of unrelenting contention—an argument culture. The argument culture urges us to approach the world—and the people in it—in an adversarial frame of mind. It rests on the assumption that opposition is the best way to get anything done."*
>
> —Deborah Tannen
> *The Argument Culture: Moving from Debate to Dialogue*

Have you ever noticed how often conversations contain war metaphors. Attack imagery is a very common occurrence in our conversation style. Getting "shot down", or "taking a stab at it", are two examples that carry strong imagery. We use terminology that is better associated with a battle or a game rather than a meeting of the minds. If we use war imagery we are likely to think of ourselves as warriors on some noble quest that might just leave bodies lying about if that is what is needed to win.

Winning and losing appears to be the only thing that matters. Being aggressive is seen as a virtue even when it is applied in situations where it isn't needed. Being less confrontational is seen as a weakness even when it is a more effective way to resolve issues of great importance.

It is as though we are somehow required to make others wrong in order to prove ourselves right. We respond to the ideas of others through criticism, opposition, or even attack rather than respectful listening and dialogue.

Deborah Tannen uses the word "agonism" to define our argumentative form of idea bashing that is so common in modern society. An agonistic response to others is basically a programmed contentiousness where we unthinkingly argue with others in order to accomplish our own objectives even when it isn't required. Agonism is not about being passionately engaged in some emotional issue. Agonism is about having a spirit of maliciousness that taints ones dealings with others.

It is as though there can only be one side to any issue and of course only one side can be right. Through experience we have learned that two sided responses to issues are woefully inadequate if we are going to truly make the right decision. There is seldom only one right answer to any issue.

Unfortunately, agonism leads to a break down of community. How can someone have a sense of community when they are so wrapped up in their own polarized opinions that they haven't taken the time to understand others? Looking for the wrongness in others doesn't lend itself to an environment of community.

If you are looking for proof of agonism in modern society, you might begin by observing journalistic style today. Conflict and dissent are all we hear or see from those that are providing us with a supposedly unbiased view of the goings on in the world. Ask yourself whether our journalists are truly unbiased. Also look at the war metaphors they use to inform the public. When was the last time you saw a journalist applauded for their non-argumentative and professional facilitative style?

Our legal system is another example of a system that stresses winning above the truth. Here again we have two sides that are pitted against each other. There is no middle ground, no compromise, only right and wrong. Instead of dueling with swords or pistols, our lawyers duel with words. Our legal system is adversarial in nature. The lawyer who shows no mercy, who attacks ferociously, is the one most admired by their colleagues. Civility, compromise, and justice aren't what our judicial system is all about. The system is about advocacy and winning at all costs.

When you live in a culture that glamorizes aggressive behavior you end up losing trust in others. You can lose trust in your organization. Many talented leaders are opting out of public office because of the caustic and intrusive critiques they are bombarded with. Unfair and demeaning treatment of those that have good intentions and a desire to serve others is their reward.

So what does agonism cost us? We learn not to trust others and we embrace a *them versus us* mentality. We never really get to the point where we feel we're a part of a community. We don't get to know others the way we should because we are polarized around important issues. We tend to run, hide, or act aggressively ourselves when faced with the aggressive behavior of others. Finally, we become desensitized to a fear driven culture that keeps us from sharing our thoughts and ideas with others.

How do we get past agonism and into dialogue? First, don't be afraid to express your convictions even when others disagree. You can disagree with others without being disagreeable. Second, remember that it is okay for the other person to disagree with you.

We are all entitled to our opinion. Listen to what they have to say and try to understand why they feel the way they do. Third, stand up for your beliefs. If someone is being malicious, tell him or her about it if you feel it will do any good. Ask yourself whether the issue is worth pursuing, if not, find something better to do with your time. And finally, be aware of your surroundings. What type of language are you being exposed too. Be a change agent. Be the person who builds trust, who builds a sense of community, and who others are willing to follow.

MEETINGS

The illuminated leader understands the value of prolific communication. One of the greatest challenges leaders face today is getting their people to express themselves. This is especially important when people meet to address critical issues.

Community circles of the past were an effective way to get people to share their thoughts. In community circles, everyone was encouraged to speak the truth. Over the years, community circles have given way to boardrooms. That trend has often curtailed rather than enhanced communication.

Where circles allow everyone to make eye contact, boardrooms are set up so that all eyes are focused mainly upon the leader. Quite often, eye contact with others in the boardroom is impossible without acrobatic maneuvering. Effectiveness often becomes the victim of efficiency. Even when agendas are flawlessly followed, the real issues lay hidden behind non-threatening conversation because anything else would be impolitic.

Meeting with others can be very complicated. Some meetings are very cordial, some entertaining, some threatening, while others are a waste of everyone's time. Groupthink is alive and well in many organizations. Getting along at meetings, being loyal to the team, is more important than addressing the organizational survival issues that need addressing.

Meetings haven't changed much in the last 200 years. There is a meeting leader, an agenda, a note-taker, and pre-arranged seating. The really creative meetings are the ones that include decorations, colorful handouts, and some type of food. It is as though everyone read the same book on how to run an efficient meeting. Still, the best managed meetings seldom extract what people are truly thinking.

One of the best books published on how to conduct effective meetings is *Sacred Circles* by Robin Deen Carnes and Sally Craig. Sacred circles are how our ancestors met and how some very effective groups meet today.

Cross-culturally we've learned meeting basics that are required to make a circle meeting work. To be successful, circle meetings share the following themes:

- *Each person takes a turn speaking* while the others listen. There should be no interruption while a person is talking. It is recommended that the person speaking say how they feel rather than generalizing about others.
- *Listen without an agenda.* Most of us listen with an agenda. When we listen with an agenda we aren't really listening, we're evaluating. You don't have to agree with what someone is saying; you just have to accept what is being said is their reality.
- *Rotate leadership* even though it will be discomforting to others. We are accustomed to the old patriarchal/military model. This model has served us well. The old model does not lend itself to great leaps of personal or organizational creativity. This is a great way to get others to invest in and take some ownership in the group.

- *Confidentiality must be maintained* for trust to develop within the group. Without trust there will never be true sharing of ideas or feelings. You should never talk to others about members of the group. If you have something to say to someone, say it to their face.
- *Take responsibility for your own needs* rather than expecting the group to be mind readers. Unless you have a psychic in the group you need to express your concerns so they can be addressed.
- *Assess your group* on a regular basis. Communities that work self-observe on a regular basis. Set up an annual meeting to address how your group is doing. Minor adjustments are needed periodically in the best of groups.

These themes exemplify how circle meetings should be held. The easiest part of conducting a circle meeting is forming a circle. After forming the circle, it gets a little more complicated. Learning and implementing the themes associated with circle meetings is the difficult part of the process. Once that is accomplished, who knows what a great leader might be able to achieve?

Action plan for communicating more effectively:

- Smile.
- Spend more time listening than talking.
- Suspend judgment.
- Ask questions.
- Listen for feelings and emotion
- Beware of smart-talkers.
- Use plain language.
- Bring your heart into the conversation.
- Speak the truth.
- Everyone is entitled to their opinion – including you.

Reflective Thoughts

4

Character

"People grow through experience if they meet life honestly and courageously. This is how character is built."

—Eleanor Roosevelt (1884 - 1962)

"Character cannot be developed in ease and quiet. Only through experience of trial and suffering can the soul be strengthened, ambition inspired, and success achieved."

—Helen Keller (1880 - 1968)

"People seem not to see that their opinion of the world is also a confession of their character."

—Ralph Waldo Emerson (1803 - 1882)

Character is the set of qualities that make someone distinctive. It is a person's character that makes them unique and interesting. Character is a combination of multiple traits or attributes that are built over time and acquired through experience. Our character defines who we are. Illuminated leaders share many traits that set them apart from ordinary leaders.

The character traits of illuminated leaders vary but they have many traits in common. As an example, illuminated leaders tend to be very passionate about what they do. They bring their *passion* to work every day. Their passion drives them to become experts and their expertise gives them power and influence.

Illuminated leaders are typically in a state of *flow* or harmony when they are focused on a specific goal and are in a state of deep concentration. Time becomes irrelevant as they focus on the work they love. What others see as problematic, the illuminated leader sees as opportunity.

Celebration is encouraged by the illuminated leader because it reinforces desired behaviors. Fun and humor are valued and encouraged so that they become part of the organizations culture. An atmosphere of *exuberance* and festivity pervades the domain of the illuminated leader.

The illuminated leader values and encourages *creative* thinking. Daydreaming and silliness are seen as value-added behaviors. Creative thinking and idea generation are supported and rewarded. The illuminated leader understands that creativity is a prerequisite to organizational survival.

Through *resonance*, the illuminated leader brings out the best in others. Positive emotional attachment to their people ensures loyalty. The illuminated leader is the emotional guide to whom others look for assurance.

The illuminated leader is a *fully engaged* person. They are a high energy person living a balanced life that includes beneficial *rituals*. They understand the need to balance the physical, emotional, mental and spiritual aspects of life. Time is set aside for renewal, play and reflective thinking.

MAKING MUSIC

I had the opportunity of sitting in on a rather unusual team training event. I found it to be a real eye opener on several levels. I was invited to attend a rehearsal of the Columbus Symphony Orchestra along with a team of managers. This was a team building initiative quite different from any I had experienced before.

I found the invitation too bizarre to turn down. My role was to connect the rehearsal to the concept of team building and share my thoughts with a dedicated group of individuals.

As it turned out, this was one of the most exciting training experiences I ever had. I took three full pages of notes on how the rehearsal had applications for anyone that was part of a team.

Understanding how teams work is critical for every leader. Joseph Jaworski in his book "Synchronicity" points out that "Increasingly, hierarchies are weakening, and institutions of all sorts, from multinational corporations to school systems, work through informal networks and self-managed teams that form, operate, dissolve, and re-form."

This was definitely the case with the Columbus Symphony Orchestra. The conductor that day was actually a guest conductor and the assistant conductor of the Chicago Symphony Orchestra.

It is difficult enough to understand the desires of our leaders when they are with us for an extended period of time. How would most of us deal with a leader who is only with us for a few days? I found the situation interesting as I listened to the cacophony that erupted from the stage as the musicians tuned dozens of instruments.

If the practice didn't go well, would the musicians blame the guest conductor? When things go poorly it is not unheard of to blame the situation on leaders, thus avoiding personal responsibility. After all, we do tend to obsess with how our leaders behave and with how they interact with their followers.

If leadership is about shaping the future of our organizations, it is imperative that people give their best to the team. Being a victim of circumstance has no real value. Placing blame only dilutes our effectiveness.

The orchestra fell silent just before they began playing the works of Wolfgang Amadeus Mozart and Dmitry Shostakovich. As I listened to their music, I also took the following notes which I feel have application for any team:

- The entire theatre was designed to focus on the musicians. How appropriate it was to focus on those that are really doing the work.
- The guest conductor addressed everyone with great respect and admiration. It was obvious that he was aware of their talent.
- Change was constant. Throughout the practice, the musicians constantly made changes through annotations to their sheet music.
- Everyone knew who was in charge. The conductor was visibly elevated and the musicians formed a half-circle around him. Everyone could see the conductor and the conductor could see everyone in the orchestra.
- There was constant feedback throughout the practice. The conductor and the musicians dialogued every time a piece of music was completed. There was some serious verbal and non-verbal communication taking place. The entire orchestra communicated constantly.
- Everyone had sheet music. Both the conductor and musicians knew what was expected of them. The instructions were clear and precise.
- The conductor was actively involved in the music. He literally danced on the stage as the musicians interpreted his vision of each piece of the concerto.
- Every musician was equal in value. No person or instrument held greater value than another. They all contributed to the musical confluence.
- The conductor perceived the tiniest flaws. He knew exactly what was expected and could tell immediately when something wasn't right.
- Musicians were positioned based upon merit. The musicians knew exactly where they stood in relation to their abilities as compared to others.

- Musicians were grouped together based upon their field of expertise. Violinists sat and worked together as a team as did the flutists. They were separate yet part of the whole.

After the practice we had the opportunity to talk to the conductor. He shared with us the challenges he faced as a guest conductor. He didn't know the people he was working with or their abilities but he did know the music and the results he expected.

One of the keys to the success of the orchestra was their willingness to practice, practice, practice, and then perform for the audience. Another key was their willingness to come to work with the expertise needed to do the job. Finally, their success came from a desire to learn from the conductor and from the other musicians that share the same overwhelming passion for their end product, the music.

FLOW

> "A person can make himself happy, or miserable, regardless of what is actually happening "outside," just by changing the contents of consciousness. We all know individuals who can transform hopeless situations into challenges to be overcome, just through the force of their personalities. This ability to persevere despite obstacles and setbacks is the quality people most admire in others, and justly so; it is probably the most important trait not only for succeeding in life, but for enjoying it as well."
>
> —Mihaly Csikszentmihalyi
> *Flow: The Psychology of Optimal Experience*

According to Csikszentmihalyi, optimal experience, also known as "flow," is when our attention can be freely invested to achieve our goals without disorder or any type of threat to defend against. Flow is when we are in harmony with the world, when our senses are focused on a specific goal and we are in a state of deep concentration consciousness.

The symbols of happiness in our culture include wealth, status and power. These symbols are based upon a concern of how others think of us. In actuality, our quality of life should not depend on what others think, but rather, how we feel about ourselves. Affluence is nice, but the correlation between wealth and well-being is highly overrated. We've all heard the term, "the person with the most *toys* wins," maybe we should alter the saying to read, "The person with the most *joys* wins."

We garner enjoyment from a sense of accomplishment. A project that challenges us, a great game of tennis or some other physical activity, a game of chess or some challenging cerebral activity, a book that captures our interest or time spent in a garden. Enjoyable activities can provide an enjoyable flow experience. Csikszenthmihalyi believes enjoyment has eight major components. These components are:

- First, the experience usually occurs when we confront tasks we have a chance of completing.
- Second, we must be able to concentrate on what we are doing.
- Third and fourth, the concentration is usually possible because the task undertaken has clear goals and provides immediate feedback.
- Fifth, one acts with deep but effortless involvement that removes from awareness the worries and frustrations of everyday life.
- Sixth, enjoyable experiences allow people to exercise a sense of control over their actions.
- Seventh, concern for the self disappears; yet paradoxically the sense of self emerges stronger after the flow experience is over.
- Eighth, the sense of the duration of time is altered; hours pass by in minutes, and minutes can stretch out to seem like hours.

When you put all these elements together there is a sense of deep enjoyment that justifies the expenditure of time needed to enter into a state of flow. Flow takes place when we are so involved in an activity that we do not appear as separate from the activity we are performing. Our efforts transition into effortlessness. We forget the unpleasant aspects of our lives and concentrate on that which brings us joy.

Effortlessness becomes timelessness when in a state of flow. Time is rendered irrelevant. Sometimes the reverse is true as evidenced by athletes who effortlessly make that impossible shot, goal, or move, in a fraction of a second. When asked, they often say that time stood still.

Flow is cross-cultural, even those who live in the most inhospitable surroundings have learned to sing, dance, and enter into enjoyable activities. Some of the most beautiful artwork comes from the bleakest parts of the globe.

There are numerous stories of how individuals who have been lost in places such as Antarctica or even imprisoned, find ways to enjoy their struggle rather than succumb to what others would consider an impossible ordeal. Some believe the most important trait of survivors is a non-self-conscious individualism, or a strongly directed purpose that is not self-seeking.

A person can be happy, or miserable, regardless of their situation by changing their mind. Perseverance over obstacles and setbacks is a choice that can make the difference between a lifetime of failure or success. Enjoying life is an option and it is the person with the most joys who wins.

CELEBRATION

> *"Values decay without attention; celebrations are one way of raising people's consciousness about the values that drive the business. Celebrating corporate heroes and heroines for their contributions to the business reinforces desired behaviors."*
>
> —Kevin and Jackie Freiberg
> *Nuts: Southwest Airlines' Crazy Recipe for Business and Personal Success*

Celebrations are an important part of organizational culture. To create a culture where celebrations are venerated, surround yourself with gregarious people. Have you ever tried to celebrate a special event with a group of negaholics? It just doesn't work. Who would want to hang around with a bunch of belligerents anyway? Not me, they drain our energy and the vitality of an organization.

Kevin and Jackie Freiberg in *Nuts: Southwest Airlines' Crazy Recipe for Business and Personal Success*, explain that Southwest targets the selection of new hires for a special kind of spirit. Southwest specifically looks for people who are a perfect fit for their culture. They are looking for people who understand and participate in organizational celebrations.

Even in their interview process, prospective employees are typically asked, "Tell me how you recently used your sense of humor in a work environment? Tell me how you have used humor to defuse a difficult situation?" Fun and humor are attitudes that are intricately linked to a spirit of celebration. Herb Kelleher who founded Southwest Airlines explains:

> *"We look for attitudes: people with a sense of humor who don't take themselves too seriously. We'll train you on whatever it is you have to do, but the one thing Southwest cannot change in people is inherent attitudes."*

Organizational values are linked directly to culture. At Southwest Airlines, it is obvious that one important value is having fun. In any company where play, humor, sharing, and laughter abound, fun is the cultural norm. When fun is the norm, celebration is a way of life.

Kevin and Jackie Freiberg provide an interesting explanation of the importance of celebration:

> *"After observing the joy and aliveness exhibited by people at Southwest Airlines, we have concluded that the cost of not responding to the human desire for celebration is very high. Celebration enhances our humanity. Without celebration, we are robbed of life and vitality that energizes the human spirit. Latent and undeveloped though it may be, there is within our nature as human beings an inherent need to sing, dance, love, laugh, mourn, tell stories, and celebrate. Whether we are talking about people in Africa,*

Australia, Asia, Europe, or the Americas, there is no culture in the world that doesn't embrace some form of festivity. To deny our need to celebrate is to deny a part of what it means to be human."

World-class organizations continuously celebrate their people, their accomplishments, their achievements, and even their failures. Celebrations are a way of saying we love what we do, how we do it, and who we are. Celebrations are literally adult versions of playground time. They energize us while allowing us to build relationships in an environment of fun and exuberance.

So what are some of the payoffs for organizations that are hearty partiers? According to the Frieberg's, it's difficult to draw a direct cause-and-effect link between productivity and profitability, yet Southwest's experience demonstrates that celebration has a number of benefits including:

- Celebration provides an opportunity for building relationships
- Celebration gives us a sense of history
- Celebration helps us envision the future
- Celebration is a way of recognizing major milestones
- Celebration reduces stress
- Celebration inspires motivation and reenergizes people
- Celebration builds self-confidence and removes fear
- Celebration helps us mourn the losses associated with change

Leaders who see celebrations as frivolous just don't get it. They mistakenly believe fun is inappropriate in the workplace. "What more do you want, we just had Hawaiian shirt day." When we annually spend three billion dollars a year on stress related health issues in the United States, fun, play and celebration should immediately come to mind as a way to de-stress our most valuable resource, our people.

EXUBERANCE

"Exuberant people take in the world and act upon it differently than those who are less lively and less energetically engaged. They hold their ideas with passion and delight, and they act upon them with dispatch. Their love of life and of adventure is palpable. Exuberance is a peculiarly pleasurable state, and in that pleasure is power."

—Kay Redfield Jamison
Exuberance: The Passion for Life

Exuberance is closely connected to feelings of joy. Being around a person who is joyful in nature is infectious. One person who possesses an exuberant spirit can typically be a very positive influence on an entire group. The very best leaders share their joyful passion with their followers and the benefits to the organization can be profound.

Our evolutionary history links exuberance with joy and play. As children we regularly expressed our joy through play. As we age we tend to put away childish pleasures and take on the more serious role of adulthood. Less play, less exuberance and less joy are often associated with growing up. Life doesn't have to be that way. There is room for playfulness in all of our lives.

Play is linked to creativity and anyone who spends any time with children quickly comes to the realization that childhood is replete with examples of unbridled creativity. Creativity is just one byproduct of exuberant playfulness. Further, studies show that a positive mood increases both creativity and flexibility in thinking.

Parents can attest to how the exuberance of their children decreases as they near adulthood. The invitations to parents to play games and participate in child like pleasures unfortunately diminish over time, yet; adults fail to grasp how exuberance has fled from their own lives and has been replaced with more sophisticated interests.

Many adults still embrace certain forms of exuberant behavior. The extroverts of the world are often known for their childlike and infectious enthusiasm. They actively engage with others while bringing a great deal of energy into the workplace. Extroverts are typically happy people and are often chosen for leadership positions over their less socially active introverted peers. Additionally, extroverts also bring a spirit of innovation and creativity into the workplace.

Exuberance has been a distinguishing trait of many great leaders. Jamison sites several leaders who were known for their exuberant behavior. One famous exuberant leader was Teddy Roosevelt who was known for his joyful and passionate nature. His ideas were energetically expressed through his love of life and nature. Life for Teddy Roosevelt was passionately experienced much the same way a child looks forward to opening presents on Christmas morning. Every day was experienced as another day of unparalleled enthusiasm. His unbridled enthusiasm had a positive impact on all those he came in contact with. Concerning Roosevelt, Jamison explains:

> *"The White House rang out not only with laughter but with the squeals of children and the clattering of their ponies going up and down the marble stairs of the presidential mansion. Roosevelt was frequently to be found chasing or being chased by his children and their animals around the White House grounds. 'You must always remember,' said a British diplomat, 'the President is about six'."*

Roosevelt's exuberance was put to good use when he used it constructively to conserve vast areas of the American wilderness. He may be one of the finest examples of how a joyful and passionate disposition can be used to great benefit. Thank goodness there are adults who are willing to express their inner child.

Exuberant people help energize the workplace. They express their ideas with heartfelt passion and delight. Their love of life and adventure is experienced anew every day and in that experience we are positively influenced. As leaders we must treasure the exuberance of others. These are the people than help to energize the workplace and in their energy we find creativity and innovation that might not be found otherwise.

CREATIVITY

This is the age of creativity because that's where information technology wants us to go next. The Nomura Research Institute, a leading think-tank and systems integrator in Japan, classified four eras of economic activity. The first three are the agricultural, the industrial and the informational. The fourth era is the age of creativity.

Why creativity? Because we place such a high value on knowledge and creativity adds value to knowledge.

John Kao in his book *Jamming* says that we are moving beyond preoccupation with the physical and financial to a concern for the purely human: imagination, ingenuity and initiative. Creative people run best on the high octane fuels of play and freedom.

There are several attributes that support flexible organizations, organizations that stand out as being creative and innovative. One attribute is that creative organizations encourage play, daydreaming, and even silliness. How is it where you work?

Clay Carr in his book, *The Competitive Power of Constant Creativity* says:

> *"If the organization has no room for play and silliness now, introducing spontaneity will certainly challenge you, particularly in that most people will see it as just 'goofing off.' If you've been frowning on individuals or groups that seemed to be having too much fun, you can stop. When someone contributes a joke or silly comment that breaks the tension or directs everyone's attention to more productive channels, recognize the wisdom in the wit. You might want to have an experienced 'humor consultant' work with your senior leadership group."*

So where do we turn to find organizations that are creative? Where do the lines between work and play evaporate? Should we benchmark an IBM or AT&T? What about a very successful marketing or advertising firm? Certainly these are places where you would expect creativity to be nurtured.

This may sound strange, but I think a great place to observe creativity is in a kindergarten class. I can attest to this because I visited my children's classes several times when they were in kindergarten. I specifically remember visiting my son's class years ago during a birthday celebration.

I noticed that everyone in his class worked and played in the same room. I wonder what effect that has on communications. I also noticed that there were lots of colorful displays hanging on the walls. It looked as though a rainbow had exploded in the room and the resulting effect was stimulating.

There were posters with the kid's names on them that praised them for their many successes. There were stars next to names and displays that exhibited the proud work of their creators for all to see.

Everyday the children gather together to share a treat of some kind. And every day they have time set aside to just play. Maybe the concept of recess should be implemented in business; it seems to work fine in kindergarten.

The rules and values the children live by are posted in extra large print and in bright colors for everyone to see. Everyday they gather together to listen to a story. The story is followed by an avalanche of questions that are each answered in turn.

My son Sage was given a birthday crown and the class sang happy birthday to him while his proud dad sang along. Everyone feasted on ice cream and congratulated him on his upcoming sixth birthday. I know he enjoyed being recognized by his friends because we talked about it that same evening at dinner.

The energy of five year old children is amazing. The creativity level is off the charts. Where else can you find purple trees, dragons, birthday kings and queens, and seemingly unlimited questions and ideas?

To be more creative we need the high octane fuel of play and freedom. I know the kids in the kindergarten class were definitely on a creative high and I walked away with some of it myself.

It would probably be a great idea to visit some Fortune 500 companies to see how they are dealing with issues related to the new creative age. But I also know that there are a lot of lessons that can be learned by visiting a kindergarten class.

CREATIVE THINKING

One of the characteristics that separate those we consider to be geniuses from others is their habit of thinking of problems in many different ways, using trial and error, rather than thinking in reproductive or old ways. It is reproductive thinking that forms rigidity of thought and directs us towards the past in order to solve problems that are better solved with new, rather than old thought processes.

According to Michael Michalko in his book *Cracking Creativity*, "If you always think the way you've always thought, you'll always get what you always got-the same old, same old ideas."

A commonly used example of reproductive thinking takes us back to the year 1968 when the Swiss dominated the watch industry. The Swiss invented the electronic watch movement at their research institute in Neuchtel, Switzerland. Even though they invented the electronic watch, it was still rejected by every Swiss watch manufacturer.

Based on their experience in the industry, they believed the electronic watch couldn't possibly be the watch of the future. After all, it was battery powered, did not have bearings or a mainspring, and had almost no gears. Seiko took one look at this invention that the Swiss manufacturers rejected at the World Watch Congress that year and literally took over the world watch market.

The Swiss example of reproductive thinking is more common than we care to admit. Business is filled with examples of creative opportunities that were rejected in large part due to the unwillingness or inability to grasp the significance of a creative idea. UNIVAC and IBM couldn't grasp the possibility that a personal computer might be a marketable commodity. They refused to accept an idea that, until then, had no foundation in their reality of what computers were for. They saw only scientific and business applications for computers. Yet we've all experienced the changes that were brought about because Apple didn't limit itself to the self-imposed limitations of reproductive thinking.

Another example of how we self-impose barriers on our limitless capability to be creative dates back to 1899 when Charles Duell, the director of the U.S. Patent Office, suggested that the government close the office because everything that could be invented had been invented. Duell's way of thinking runs counter to how geniuses such as Thomas Edison approached creativity.

We can attribute Thomas Edison's genius in part to his immense productivity and his willingness to see the possibility in others ideas. Edison still holds the record of 1,093 patents. He guaranteed his productivity and the productivity of his employees by setting idea quotas. His personal quota was one minor invention every ten days and a major invention every six months.

This is pretty progressive thinking for a time when we still lit our homes by candlelight and the primary mode of transportation involved the use of horses rather than automobiles. And after all these years, I doubt that very few organizations actually set idea quotas for their employees. Yet today, more than ever before, we need to set idea quotas in order to compete in this *Age of Creativity*.

So how do we do this? Do we just demand our people be more creative? Do we set a quota on creativity? Of course not; how can we expect our people to be more creative if we haven't taught them some basic skills that allow them to tap into their potential? That would be no different than sending someone out to repair an automobile without a toolkit.

Short courses on brainstorming will not hack-it anymore. Instead, we need to teach our people how to use an entire toolkit of creativity enhancing tools much like the ones author Michael Michalko identifies in his book *Thinkertoys* or *Cracking Creativity: The Secrets of Creative Genius*. Studies have shown that being a creative genius has less to do with high IQ than it does with observation, curiosity, productivity, and some really good creativity enhancing tools.

Book stores are loaded with books on how to be more creative. Check out the stores and make creative thinking a personal goal. New ideas are needed now more than ever and solving problems is a great way to put your creativity to work.

NATURE

> *"Nature organizes much more effectively than we humans do, and quite differently. For example, life works cooperatively, not competitively, in networks of relationships where each depends on the other."*
>
> —Margaret J. Wheatley
> *Turning to One Another*

Nature is the physical world including all natural phenomena and living things. Nature is also seen as the intrinsic or essential qualities of somebody or something.

If we traveled through time, we would see ancient cultures communing with nature through myths and rituals. The ancients were in rhythm with nature and used calendars as a sacred pathway through life. Their life's path included a multitude of rituals and celebrations that flowed with the seasons.

We celebrate nature today in our own unique ways. In the modern world we use technology to track our pathway through life. We attempt to organize our lives as effectively as nature but our attempts typically fall short of our desired outcomes. Instead of embracing nature and the lessons it holds we use screen savers that remind us of the natural world that exists far from our place of work. We also use color coded calendars that set a rhythm suited for hectically communing in the business environment rather than the rhythm of the changing seasons.

Illuminated leaders understand the nature of nature. They understand that life is part of nature and it is meant to be cooperative and non-competitive. They also understand that nature is about networks of relationships where we depend upon each other to reach our full potential.

According to Frances Bernstein, *Classical Living: Reconnecting with the Rituals of Ancient Rome*, "In the Roman sacred calendar from January to December, we note periods of beginnings, growth, nurturing, ripening, and dying—only to begin again." She goes on to say:

> *"Winter brings the period of birth when sunlight is born again at the winter solstice. The yearly cycle proceeds then through spring, the period of growth; summer, the period of attainment; and autumn, the period of death and endings."*

The cycles of the year are a metaphor for life. Each month carries its own special meaning. How we view the months and the natural changes they represent comes largely from our ancestral past and personal experiences. Here is my own idiosyncratic view of the months of the year, their meaning and my way of celebration:

- January is about the New Year and new beginnings. It is the month for making life-altering changes. Funny hats and noisemakers are optional.
- February is a time of purification and cleansing. It is also a time for renewing romantic relationships and expressing love.
- March is a time of creativity and self-discovery. It is also a time of rebirth and new beginnings.
- April brings with it the promise of new growth. The birds return from warmer climates as frost gives way to the warm rays of the sun. Lawn equipment is dusted off and put in working order.
- May is the time for blossoming and growth. It is a time to honor mothers and all that is feminine. The loss of loved ones is mourned and those who sacrificed their lives for our freedom are honored.
- June is a time to nurture ideas and relationships. Fathers are honored as is the flag and all it symbolizes. Tents are pulled from storage and canoe trips are contemplated and sometimes taken.
- July is steeped in family activities and patriotism. It is a time of recreation and playfulness. The joy of a well aimed water balloon is experienced and undying gratitude is given to the person who invented air conditioning.
- August is a time of retreat and reflection upon the abundance of life. It is a time for new learning and growth. Summer activities fade and preparations are made for the new school year.
- September is a time for closure and renewal. It is a time of transition. The glory of summer gives way to the glory of autumn.

- October is a reminder of how things change. Hopefully the passing of time has also seen personal growth and improvements. It is a time for beautifully colored leaves, bonfires and watching old movies about ghosts in wishing wells (Abbott and Costello).

- November is a time for giving thanks for a multitude of blessings. It is a time for feasts and rejoicing. Television reveals helium filled balloons floating along the streets of New York City while the family eats donuts and sips hot chocolate. The men and women who serve and have served our nation are honored for their sacrifices to the nation.

- December is a time of sharing. It is a time for family and friends. This month is filled with festivities, abundance, celebrations, gifts, and a spirit of peace. It is a time to remember that our journey through this world is infinitely more enjoyable when shared with our loved ones. Ornaments are placed on the house and tree and the genius of Charles Dickens (A Christmas Carol) is enjoyed.

Illuminated leaders understand that nature and the rituals associated with it are important. Nature is best observed both inside and outside the workplace. What are your rituals? Do they flow with the seasons? Do you use rituals to celebrate special occasions and the passage of time?

Observing and being part of nature brings about much needed balance. Just like the ancients, Illuminated leaders understand nature and the importance of rituals associated with nature. Cooperation, non-competiveness, networks and relationships are all lessons we can take from nature.

RESONANCE

> *"Leaders have always played a primordial emotional role. No doubt humankind's original leaders—whether tribal chieftains or shamanesses—earned their place in large part because their leadership was emotionally compelling. Throughout history and in cultures everywhere, the leader in any human group has been the one to whom others look for assurance and clarity when facing uncertainty or threat, or when there's a job to be done. The leader acts as the group's emotional guide."*

> —Daniel Goleman, Richard Boyatzis and Annie McGee
> *Primal Leadership*

The authors explain when leaders drive emotions in a positive way they bring out the best in their followers. They call this effect *resonance*. When emotions are driven in a negative way, the effect is called *dissonance*. They go on to say, "Whether an organization withers or flourishes depends to a remarkable extent on the leaders' effectiveness in this primal emotional dimension."

When you look at who people want to work for, it becomes evident that we are drawn towards resonance and away from dissonance. It is the emotionally intelligent leader who attracts talented people. The resonant leader is a joy to be around. These are the people who make it okay to laugh, smile, and be genuine. They exude feelings of warmth and compassion. These are the people who like other people. They enjoy helping, mentoring, and making a positive difference wherever they go.

And does this type of leader have an impact on retention of talented people? Of course they do. We like being around enthusiastic and optimistic leaders. In fact, when making the decision to stay with one organization over another organization, emotional attachment will often win out over a pay increase or other benefits. This is particularly true when work is emotionally demanding.

A leader who is supportive and empathetic can greatly impact the climate (for the better) within their organization. These leaders are largely responsible for the perceptions of others. Dissonant leaders also impact their organization but in a different way. The dissonant leader brings toxicity to the workplace. According to Goleman, Boyatzis and McGee:

> *"Wherever they go in an organization, the legacy of their tenure marks a telltale trail of de-motivation and apathy, anger and resentment. In short, dissonant leaders are the bosses that people dread working for."*

Truthfully, very few if any people are born resonant leaders. Having a positive emotional impact on people takes time and great effort. The path of the leader is often strewn with mistakes and false starts. In fact, the higher a leader moves up the organization, the fuzzier the landscape becomes. Leaders are often protected from the reality that surrounds them. They receive less accurate feedback and important information is often withheld.

One of the best ways to excel as a resonant leader is to spend time with people. Listen to them, talk with them, and share your ideas with them. When we spend time with others we break down the invisible barriers that often lead to discord and disharmony.

Leaders cannot become emotional guides if they have no emotional attachment to their people. Emotional attachment can only take place once a relationship has been created. If you pay close attention to a leader who brings resonance to their organization, you will see a person who understands and practices relationship building. The opposite holds true for the leader who embodies the attributes of dissonance.

FULL ENGAGEMENT

"We live in digital time. Our rhythms are rushed, rapid fire and relentless, our days carved up into bits and bytes. We celebrate breadth rather than depth, quick reaction more than considered reflection. We skim across the surface, alighting for brief moments at dozens of destinations but rarely remaining for long at any one. We race through our lives without pausing to consider who we really want to be or where we really want to go. We're wired up but we're melting down."

—Jim Loehr and Tony Schwartz
The Power of Full Engagement

Loehr and Schwartz are adamant that energy, not time, is the fundamental currency of high performance. "The skillful management of energy, individually and organizationally, makes possible something that we call full engagement."

It is their belief that to be fully engaged, we must be physically energized, emotionally connected, mentally focused and spiritually aligned with a purpose beyond our immediate self-interest. Being fully engaged means feeling eager to get to work in the morning and just as happy to return home in the evening. It is a great day when you can fully immerse yourself in your work and your family, yet how often does that happen?

Illuminated leaders draw upon four separate but related sources of energy. These sources of energy include the physical, emotional, mental and spiritual. They are interconnected and have a profound effect on each other. To be fully engaged we must effectively use all of these sources of energy. To be physically fit yet emotionally, mentally or spiritually disturbed does not allow a person to reach their full potential. We must work towards an energy balance that embraces the physical, emotional, mental and spiritual.

Loehr and Schwartz go on to explain that the primary markers of physical capacity are strength, endurance, flexibility and resilience. These are precisely the same markers that apply to emotional, mental, and spiritual capacity.

Emotional flexibility reflects the capacity to move freely and appropriately along a wide spectrum of emotions rather than responding rigidly or defensively. Emotional resilience is the ability to bounce back from experiences of disappointment, frustration and even loss.

It is understood that mental endurance is a measure of the ability to sustain focus and concentration over time. Mental flexibility is marked by the capacity to move between the rational and the intuitive and to embrace multiple points of view.

Our spiritual strength is reflected in the commitment to one's deepest values, regardless of circumstance and even when adhering to them involves personal sacrifice. Spiritual flexibility reflects the tolerance for values and beliefs that are different than one's own, so long as those values and beliefs don't bring harm to others.

To be fully engaged requires strength, endurance, flexibility and resilience in all dimensions of the physical, emotional, mental and spiritual self. The power of full engagement can be seen in a paradigm shift from old ways of thinking to new ways of thinking. One important shift includes the concept of management of energy rather than management of time. Good time management skills are helpful but if you are exhausted to the point of collapse, what good will a leather bound time planner do you?

Here are some ideas for using and renewing our energy:

- Asking whether we are using our energy to fulfill our most important purposes in life. If we don't like our answer, it is probably time to make some changes.
- Are we in energy renewing or energy draining relationships? If we are in energy draining relationships it would be wise to ask why this is, and make appropriate changes.
- Do we have balance in our lives? Are we spending value added time on the physical, emotional, mental and spiritual aspects of our lives?
- Have we set aside time for renewal? Everyone needs to escape once in awhile. Do you regularly escape from the hustle-bustle of the world? Set aside renewal time just for yourself.
- Set aside time for playful activities. You need to do things outside of work that make you feel like a kid again. Time invested in a hobby is time well spent.

We do not have a limitless supply of energy. It is no wonder so many people break down, burn out, lose their passion, or even checkout of this world prematurely. We must invest our energy wisely so that we can accomplish those things we feel are most important in our lives. This requires a balancing act of sorts and a willingness to use and renew our energy wisely.

Illuminated leaders use their supply of energy wisely. They also watch over their followers to ensure they do not burn out, lose their passion or worse. It is the leader's responsibility to stay fully engaged, physically energized, emotionally connected, mentally focused, spiritually aligned and interconnected with others. In short, Illuminated leaders must be fully engaged.

RITUALS

Autumn has always been a very special time of year for me. I feel energized when the air takes on a slight chill and the fragrance of leaves wafts through the air. I have found autumn to be a time for personal reflection. Each year I take time from my duties at work and I re-energize at home by spending time with my wife and my children.

One ritual I thoroughly enjoyed and remember with great fondness was waiting with the kids outside in the clean crisp air as their bright yellow school bus came to carry them away to learn the things they needed to learn in school. I also waited patiently with my wife each day as the same bus brought its precious cargo safely home.

On one of those days the kids always found mom and dad waiting for them with pumpkins and carving knives. We have a pumpkin carving ritual every year that we look forward too. Fleming and Sage, my kids, love the carving part and dad somehow always ends up cleaning out the inside of the pumpkins.

We still watch movies together that allow us to share the spirit of the season. I still remember coming home from one of several business trips and watching "Its the Great Pumpkin" and "Hold That Ghost" as part of our annual Halloween film fest. Drinking hot apple cider made our time together even better.

After a week or sometimes more than a week at home, I'm still ready to head back to work feeling energized and enthused. The rituals I've shared, waiting on the bus, carving pumpkins, and watching movies that get us in the spirit of the season are all a part of clarifying the really important things in life. I believe it is the clarity that comes about through these types of rituals that energize and enthuse. Even though my children are no longer passengers on the bright yellow school bus, I think of them and our rituals every time one passes by.

We all have rituals that are an important part of who we are. We see rituals performed in churches, at work, at home, and at play. Random acts are not rituals. Rituals come about through repetitive acts of one kind or another. Rituals can be life changing, positive, and full of vibrancy. They can also be negative and hurtful if we allow ourselves to repeatedly embrace those things which are harmful to us physically, spiritually, or emotionally.

There is one ritual which very few of us perform. I know I don't perform the ritual often enough. What I'm writing about is the ritual of personal reflection. Taking the time just to sit and think about what is going on in our lives and making sure we are heading in the right direction.

A well known author and speaker, Brian Tracy, *Psychology of Achievement*, explains the importance of quiet time in order to ask ourselves the really tough questions. A ritual of reflective thinking helps us clarify our path through the complicated world in which we live.

For some, a few minutes alone in the morning without interruption gives us enough time to ponder the questions that beg answering. For others, the ritual may involve a long walk, a run, digging in the dirt, spending time in a natural setting, or even a few stolen moments alone in our car.

Regardless of where or how, I'm sure most of us would benefit from a ritual that allows us to address the types of questions that can't be answered on a multiple choice examination. These questions are best asked and answered between school bus arrivals, departures and pumpkin carving. Ten minutes of uninterrupted personal reflection time can be life changing.

Illuminated leaders take time for personal reflection. This ritual takes very little time and can be extremely effective if used regularly. The clarity that comes from personal reflection can be very energizing and over time will lead to positive life changes.

Action plan for character:

- Bring your expertise to work.
- Be passionate about what you do.
- Respect others.
- Focus your attention on your people.
- Give feedback often.
- Be in harmony with the world.
- Change your attitude by changing your mind.
- Celebrate often and embrace festivity.
- Exuberance is infectious – that is a good thing.
- Encourage playfulness – it is linked directly to creativity.
- Be observant, curious and productive.
- Create meaningful rituals.
- Get emotionally attached to your people.
- Manage your energy wisely.
- Set aside time for renewal and play.
- Take time for reflective thinking.

Reflective Thoughts

5

Inspiration

"Inspiration does exist, but it must find you working."

—Pablo Picasso

"A mediocre idea that generates enthusiasm will go further than a great idea that inspires no one."

—Mary Kay Ash

The illuminated leader is inspired and *inspires* others. They know how to bring out the very best in others. They build relationships and form friendships because they understand and value others.

They value the uniqueness of others and make it their mission to turn the workplace into a sanctuary where everyone can pour their heart into their dreams. The illuminated leader ensures *success* by turning dreams into realities through the power of positive affirmations. The illuminated leader takes full responsibility for life's outcomes moving energetically toward self-sufficiency.

Recognition of others is of paramount importance to the illuminated leader. Taking time to recognize others is seen as time well spent. Recognition happens frequently and as quickly as possible.

The illuminated leader understands that *rewards* are given to ensure certain behaviors are repeated. Rewards are linked to organizational goals and are designed for simplicity. Goals are communicated continuously and goal accomplishments are rewarded often and publicly. What gets rewarded gets done and the illuminated leader takes time to make rewards meaningful for the individual.

The illuminated leader is an inspiration to everyone around them. Their generous nature and willingness to honor the good works of others inspires legendary trust and loyalty.

INSPIRATION

"One of the greatest needs of the human spirit is to be inspired and to inspire. Inspiration is the oxygen of the soul. Inspiration comes from love, not fear—we cannot be inspired if we are not loving and loved."

—Lance Secretan
Inspire! What Great Leaders Do

According to Secretan, the most important people in history had several common characteristics. They had extraordinary clarity about their destiny, cause, and calling and aligned these fully in their lives. They knew how to serve and bring out the best in others; and had a gift for being inspired themselves. "When we are truly on purpose in our lives, our energy translates into an inspiring experience for ourselves—and therefore for others."

There is no shortage of data showing the lack of inspiration at work. A study by Towers Perrin/Gang and Gang, organizational performance experts, showed that three-quarters of those surveyed felt negatively toward their work and, of these, 28 percent were actively looking to find employment elsewhere, and, perhaps most disturbing of all, 28 percent of those most "intensely negative" planned to continue being unhappy right where they were.

Inspired people are easy to spot. Inspired people are the ones that are enthused about what they do. The word *enthuse* derives from the Greek root words meaning to be inspired and being possessed by the divine. Great leaders inspire their people through their own enthusiasm.

Everyone wants to be inspired and they want to inspire others. Through inspiration we build relationships and form friendships that can last a lifetime. Unfortunately there are many leaders that believe leadership is only about power. Power-based leadership is a form of fear-based leadership. This form of leadership is not the least bit inspiring and leaves followers feeling manipulated and controlled.

Leaders should inspire their followers. They should support and guide their people. They should make the workplace a sanctuary where we enter into healthy relationships and revere others.

Secretan explains:

"A sanctuary is a holy relationship, an association where we give reverence to all of the people and things within it. It is a group of people connected by their souls, among whom a sacred code is practiced and members live in grace, serving and honoring one another…Teams, departments, divisions, or corporations, as well as families, tribes, and clans are simply different-sized sanctuaries or communities."

So do you feel inspired? Do you inspire others? What can you do to inspire or be inspired? Secretan lists what employees really want to know:

- Do leaders care?
- Are our leaders compassionate?
- Are people more important than metrics?
- Is my career secure?
- How can I achieve greater meaning and fulfillment from my work?
- Am I being told the truth?
- Is this an organization with integrity?
- Do our leaders respect me and treat me as a spiritual being rather than just a means of production?
- Does my contribution matter?
- Are my gifts seen?

The role of every leader is to inspire their followers. When we fail to inspire we diminish our leadership potential and the potential of our people. The way to inspire is to see and acknowledge every person for the unique potential they bring to the sanctuary of the workplace.

Our role as leader is not to obtain power or to seek control over others. Our role is to unshackle the greatness of others. To do this, we must create an environment of enthusiasm and inspiration.

SUCCESS

" The secret of success is constancy to purpose."

—Benjamin, Earl of Beaconsfield Disraeli
Speech, June 24ᵗʰ, 1870

"You can have anything you want if you want it desperately enough. You must want it with an inner exuberance that erupts through the skin and joins the energy that created the world."

—Sheila Graham
Do It! Let's Get Off Our Buts

According to John-Roger and Peter McWilliams, *DO IT! Lets Get Off Our Buts,* "Emotion is necessary for sustained activity," and, "What we think about determines how we feel." Those who pour their hearts into their dreams are very likely to succeed. One reason emotionally charged people succeed is the lack of like-minded competitors. Another reason for their success is the ability to visualize the rewards of their dreams while losers tend to visualize the penalties of failure.

What is your dream? Do you think about it all the time? Do you see your dream from a perspective of success or failure? An interesting thing about humans is that we like to be right. Our egos don't like us to be wrong, therefore; if we see ourselves being successful, we get busy being successful. The bad news is that we can also get very busy being failures if that is how we visualize our dreams.

An effective technique for visualizing one's dreams is through the use of affirmations. Affirmations are positive statements that take place in the present. Affirmations are dream statements that allow us to emotionally visualize, in a present tense, our inner most desires. Affirmations should correlate directly to our personal goals. Affirmations challenge us to turn our dreams into our own personal success story.

We are constantly bombarded with negative thoughts. We tell ourselves we don't have what it takes to be successful, regardless of how we define success. We see others succeed and think that their success is okay but that can't happen to us. These thoughts are negative affirmations and act as obstacles to our success. We tend to focus our energy on our thoughts so why in the world would we want to knowingly focus on the negative when the positive is so much more appealing? Focus on your dream through positive affirmations and you will move in that direction.

Be your own navigator and take personal responsibility for your life and all the dreams that make it worth living. Happiness doesn't come through the approval of others. Your most important relationship remains the relationship you have with your self. As Lily Tomlin said, "We're all in this alone." Yes, we want and need the company of others. Relationships and all the positives they provide are important to our personal development.

Yet, there are those who do not want us to succeed. They may be jealous, or they may fear the success of others because of their own failures. It makes me wonder how many people told Thomas Edison or the Wright Brothers they were wasting their time experimenting with creations. Can you imagine some of the comments that must have been made when Edison was working on the first light bulb? "Tom, are you nuts, this will never work, just give up, and candles work just fine."

Not surprisingly, it was Thomas Edison who said, "Many of life's failures are people who did not realize how close they were to success when they gave up." Edison wasn't a quitter; he was an emotionally charged visionary who must have used positive affirmations to turn his dreams into reality.

Learn to discard negative affirmations like the corrupt baggage they are. Focus on the positive. Be thinking about your dreams all of the time. See yourself as a success in the present and always be moving toward the accomplishment of your goals. If you do this with great emotion, you'll create your own success.

CONGRATULATIONS

My son Sage decided he wanted to be on the basketball team. He's always been interested in sports and he loved basketball. We've really been lucky with Sage, he is well balanced, is good at sports, music, the arts, and academics. He was 13 when he tried out with dozens of other boys his age. We received a letter from the coach that began with the phrase, "congratulations you made the team." We were of course very happy to hear he made the team. When we read the entire letter we were surprised to read that although he was on the team there were some restrictions we found a bid odd.

- You are expected to attend all practices (every night for the whole season) (okay)
- You are expected to attend all games (sure)
- You will not under any conditions be allowed to play at a game (what?)
- You will not dress for the game but instead will sit on the bench and wear a tie (huh?)

Basically, the letter stated that he and two other boys had been designated as what was being called, "the thirteenth man." I've never been much of a sports person. I naively thought that if you made the team, you actually made the team.

My wife and I spoke to Sage about the letter and asked him if he wanted to do all the work, and spend all of the time, yet not be allowed to play a game or wear a uniform.

Sage, being Sage, was all about supporting the team and his school. I know he was hurt but his loyalty to others far exceeded his own desires. We gave him time to think about his decision to remain with the team or to spend the winter on a sport where he would be allowed to compete. His final decision was to stay with the team.

As you might imagine, I went to see the coach. I asked him to help me understand why he was running a program that was one of exclusion rather than inclusion. Didn't he know how the boys would feel if they sat on the bench and couldn't even wear a team uniform? The local football team has what appear to be one-hundred kids and most of them never play a game but they at least have uniforms.

I told the coach that even though I didn't agree with the no-play rule, I would support his decision. I also told him that I understood the thirteenth man concept if this was a way to improve performance for those who were showing potential and might have a chance in the future to play basketball. I did not understand why he would restrict the wear of a team uniform. Was there no money in the budget? I offered to pay for the three uniforms myself.

I would even go to the PTO or the school board (I was on the School Board) and get the money if needed. His answer surprised me.

"If I give the kids uniforms their parents will expect them to play and I don't want to argue with the parents."

"You've got to be kidding me!"

"I thought this was about the kids. If the parents sign an agreement that says their children will not play, they should stick to the agreement." I explained that I thought his decision was wrong-minded and that the message he was sending was one of exclusion that defeated the whole purpose of team-spirit. His answer was, "I'm the coach and I'm not changing my mind."

To add insult to injury, the next week we received a team roster. The roster was split into two parts. The first part listed the team players. They were listed in a large, bold, font with team numbers assigned. Guess how the thirteenth player(s) were listed? I practically needed a magnifying glass to read their names. The coach didn't even list the team all together on the team roster. What message did that send?

I can tell you, it didn't take my wife more than two seconds to let her feelings be known. It really didn't do any good though. Some people just aren't conscious, they just don't get it! How sad for them and those they come into contact with.

This could have easily have been an inspiring experience. Instead it became an unnecessarily negative and frustrating experience.

Congratulations, you made the team! Yeah right!

Illuminated leaders look for the talent in others and nurture that talent in caring ways. They are inclusive rather than exclusive. How silly to exclude anyone who has something to contribute to your team. Illuminated leaders are aware that they can have a positive or negative effect on the lives of others. Illuminated leaders opt to be a positive influence.

Illuminated leaders have self-monitoring skills. This means they can diagnose situations well and adapt their behavior based on social cues. They understand how their behavior affects others. They are also effective at resolving conflicts. Through self-monitoring, illuminated leaders gain and keep the support they need to run their organizations.

Sadly, Sage didn't continue with basketball even though he loved the game. He found soccer and tennis coaches who understood the concept of inclusion and who had better self-monitoring skills. They let him wear the uniform, have his name on the list of team players, and of course, play in the game. Sage was a soccer team starter and first seat singles tennis player as a high school freshman.

There is a lesson in this story for every leader. It is the illuminated leader's responsibility to bring out the light (special gifts and talents) that are in each of their followers. Don't hinder your greatest resource, rather; include everyone in your efforts. There is no middle ground when it comes to inclusion. Either you are on the team or not. Make sure your people know in every way that they are on your team.

RECOGNITION

> *"Communication combined with recognition of strategically important behaviors takes your vision and values off the wall and puts them into the hearts and minds of your people, which is exactly the place you want your vision and values to be."*
>
> —Adrian Gostick and Chester Elton
> *The Carrot Principle*

When we take the time to recognize a person or group for their good work we instill a sense of trust in the workplace. Recognition validates the value we place on our organizational vision, values, goals and objectives. Strategic recognition sends a powerful message to our people and studies consistently show that it also helps the bottom line.

How often have we received mixed messages when the wrong type of behavior is rewarded? What gets recognized and rewarded in an organization tells volumes about its culture. We may want to produce a quality product yet we reward rapid work. We say we want our people to be creative yet we demand conformity. We need risk takers yet we only recognize those who avoid risks, those who always play it safe. We ask for peoples opinions but when they express themselves openly and honestly they get shut down or worse. So what is the message we are sending? Does our message instill trust or distrust?

Almost as bad as sending the wrong message to our people is sending no message at all. A recent Gallup Poll found that 65 percent of Americans received no praise or recognition in the workplace in the past year. We all need recognition if only to confirm we are doing the right things and that our efforts are valued by others. Employees need to be valued and recognized for their contributions.

Gallup's research shows that for employees to feel valued and committed to the workplace, they need to be recognized at least weekly. This can come in the form of a simple "thank you", or something more elaborate if justified. For recognition to be effective it must be given often and it must be given with sincerity.

It is the leader's job to pay attention to what is going on in the workplace and to recognize those that are living the organizations vision, values, goals and objectives. That, in its essence is strategic recognition. Strategic recognition is both the right and the smart thing to do.

If you want to be exceptionally great at recognition, look beyond the workplace into what your people like to do outside of business hours. What are their hobbies? Do they have any special interests? Interests outside the workplace can be as varied as the talents displayed inside the workplace. Getting to know your people is an important and critical step towards effective recognition.

For those who argue that recognition can cause jealousy in the workplace you might point out the findings of Gostick and Elton in "The Carrot Principle":

> *"As we have visited teams where recognition is frequent and is aligned with core values to avoid favoritism, employees do not complain of jealousy. On the contrary, employees get more upset when recognition is rare and they are ignored."*

Can recognition be over done? Ask yourself that question. Do you feel you have been recognized too often? My guess is that you haven't been recognized too much or too often. Whether we feel we have been recognized too much or not, excessive recognition is seldom an issue. The real issue is that recognition is typically ignored or delayed.

Whenever my children played soccer I would cheer them and their team whenever they made a goal or even came close to making a goal. I've even been known, on occasion, to applaud the other team when they've made a great play. I didn't wait until after the game to cheer, that would have little or no value. We need to give recognition when the behavior we desire has taken place. Recognition has great meaning and we should give recognition to those who deserve it as often and as quickly as possible.

Strategic recognition brings many benefits to the workplace. Recognition creates trust and trust speeds up processes that in turn increase profits. We know that recognition improves performance, productivity and morale. We also know that recognition reduces employee turnover. The number one reason people leave an employer is they don't feel appreciated at work. There is also greater satisfaction with leaders who understand the value of recognition and use recognition to reward the right types of behavior.

Give recognition whenever and wherever you can. It makes a difference.

REWARDS

> *"I can live for two months on one good compliment."*
>
> —Mark Twain

The oldest management principle in the world is "what gets rewarded gets done." Yet quite often we forget to link the goals of our organization with a meaningful reward and recognition program. If we want great customer service in our organization we need to reward great customer service. If we want people to be creative and innovative we need to reward creativity and innovation. It is really that simple.

We also need to ensure that the goals we have set are perceived as realistic and achievable. Goals should allow people to stretch their intellectual muscle. If goals are too easy people will not feel challenged. If goals are too hard they won't even try, even when the rewards are tempting.

There are several criteria that are necessary to ensure we have a confluent program. One criterion is simplicity. It amazes me how difficult we make some recognition programs. If it is too difficult or time consuming for mere mortals to figure out, they will give up in frustration. In that case no one receives the recognition they deserve, so everyone loses.

Rewards can be formal or informal. A well placed pat on the back or a simple "thank you" can mean a lot to someone who has spent innumerable hours working on a special project. Informal rewards are also very likely to be timely. If it takes six months to get a formal reward approved the meaningfulness of the recognition is as suspect as the timing. On the other hand, a well timed and attended special event may be in order.

Rewards should be meaningful if they are going to have a positive impact. Sally may have been putting in over 12 hour days for months and has sacrificed time with her family and friends. If she has saved the organization thousands of dollars due to her efforts, I doubt that an exquisitely inscribed tire gauge is going to send the type of message that encourages personal sacrifice. Of course if Sally is into exquisitely inscribed tire gauges you may be right on target.

We need to communicate our goals continuously and the rewards and recognition that are achievable by reaching those goals. This can be done through staff meetings, newsletters, flyers, e-mails, or any other form of effective communication. Rewards and recognition also need to be ongoing. The very best programs offer constant and timely feedback. You may already have some great programs in your organization that need to be taken from the shelf, dusted off, and re-implemented.

I would also suggest that managers, particularly senior managers, get involved with reward and recognition programs. It is always nice to know that the boss cares and is willing to take the time and effort to recognize and reward those who are deserving.

Finally, I feel we tend to err on the side of being too frugal in the rewarding and recognition of the accomplishment of others. If we're going to err, make sure we do so by being over generous in our accolades to others. In my opinion, the oldest management principle, "what gets rewarded gets done," is as applicable today as ever.

Action plan for inspiring and being inspired:

- Be enthusiastic.
- Guide and support your people.
- Show you care.
- Build relationships and form friendships
- Treat others with respect.
- Make the workplace a sanctuary.
- Pour your heart into your dreams.
- Use positive affirmations daily.
- Take personal responsibility for your life.
- Discard negative baggage.
- Some people just aren't conscious – get over it.
- Take time to recognize the good work of others.
- Pay attention to what is going on in the workplace.
- Reward the behavior you want to see.
- You can never recognize people often enough.
- What gets rewarded gets done.
- Communicate goals continuously.
- Be generous in your accolades.

Reflective Thoughts

6
Service

"I've come to believe that each of us has a personal calling that's as unique as a fingerprint - and that the best way to succeed is to discover what you love and then find a way to offer it to others in the form of service, working hard, and also allowing the energy of the universe to lead you."

—Oprah Winfrey

"Always render more and better service than is expected of you, no matter what your task may be."

—Og Mandino

The illuminated leader knows that *service* is important to personal growth and the growth of our communities. They understand that true success is found in being of service to others. We are not meant to spend our time in isolation. We are meant to be with others, to relate to others, to be part of a community that fulfills our need for belonging and for providing service to others.

There are many ways to be of service. Illuminated leaders join clubs and associations that add value to the *community*. Volunteering for a worthy cause brings about positive outcomes far beyond our comprehension. Serving others with heartfelt sincerity is its own reward.

Being kind, generous, and considerate of others are attributes associated with illuminated leadership. When these attributes are displayed enthusiastically we embody the spirit of service. This sense of service can be seen in organizations such as the United States Air Force that acknowledges "Service Before Self" as a core value.

Accountability is an attribute serves the greater good. Illuminated leaders understand the need to empower others through freedom-based leadership.

Followers are encouraged to express their talents and creativity in ways that better serve the needs of the organization and the community.

Illuminated leaders have always served the greater good. Mother Teresa spent her life tending to the poor and destitute. Mahatma Gandhi served his fellow countrymen and relentlessly worked to gain India national independence making it the largest democracy in the world. Dr. King worked tirelessly as the heart and soul of the United States civil rights movement. These and other great leaders knew what it meant to serve and the world benefitted through their efforts.

The illuminated leader shares their unique talents with others. They make themselves accountable for the success of others and in so doing create a service based culture where it is truly better to give than to receive.

COMMUNITY

> *"To some it is a safe haven where survival is assured through mutual cooperation. To others, it is a place of emotional support, with deep sharing and bonding with close friends. Some see community as an intense crucible for personal growth. For others it is primarily a place to pioneer their dreams."*

—Corrine McLaughlin & Gordon Davidson
In the Company of Others:
Making Community in the Modern World

What is happening to community involvement in the United States? The trend is clear; we're becoming less and less involved in what takes place in our communities. Robert Putnam, a political scientist and Harvard professor provides some alarming statistics concerning the continuous decline of community related activity throughout the country.

We're spending less and less time as members of clubs and associations. We're not volunteering to help the Red Cross, Girl or Boy Scouts. Since 1973, attendance at public meetings on town or school affairs has fallen by more than a third. The decline is even more significant when you look at the numbers of people that are joining labor unions or serving on a committee of some local organization. And as a culture we've stopped going to Parent Teacher Organization meetings.

The number of people that socialize with their neighbors more than once a year has dropped down to only 61%. Where Americans have been some of the most civic minded and trusting people in the world, we are rapidly catching up with those nations that are the least civic minded and trusting. Putnam believes that America has traditionally been considered unusually "civic", yet there is striking evidence that American civil society has notably declined over the past several decades.

Scholars have searched far and wide to find some definitive reason for the downward trend in community involvement. They have looked at variables such as age, education, gender, technology and more. Some of their findings are interesting and will undoubtedly be explored at great length. Yet the trend towards less and less civic engagement continues unabated.

Putnam did share that the prime suspect for this downward trend in civic engagement and trust could be related directly to the impact of television on Americans. He states the following:

> *"In 1950 barely 10 percent of American homes had television sets, but by 1959, 90 percent did...viewing hours grew by 17-20 percent during the 1960s and by an additional 7-8 percent during the 1970s."*

He also found that television viewing increases with age and that by 1995 viewing per TV household was more than 50 percent higher than it had been in the 1950s. In addition, he explains:

> *"Most studies estimate that the average American now watches roughly four hours per day (excluding periods in which television is merely playing in the background). Even a more conservative estimate of three hours means that television absorbs 40 percent of the average Americans free time, an increase of about one-third since 1965...By the late 1980s three-quarters of all U.S. homes had more than one set, and these numbers too are rising steadily, allowing ever more private viewing."*

It would be hard to imagine life today without immediate access to the arts and entertainment at the click of a remote. Yet there is no doubt, as a society, we are spending an inordinate amount of time watching television while subsequently being stingy in allocating time to our communities. Does this mean we should give up television? That would be blasphemous to a society whose culture is so intricately linked to television. There is great value in television viewing. After a busy day it is nice to spend some time relaxing or learning something new and useful.

Of course, there is a way to tell whether we are spending too much time watching television. If you find that you are watching re-runs of the Dukes of Hazard, knowing full well that Boss Hogg is going to lose every time, you are probably watching way too much television.

Instead, give your eyes a rest and exceed the national average of community involvement. Go outside and talk to a neighbor. Join a club or organization that is of interest to you. Or, do some random act of kindness. The television set will be there when you get back. Really, no kidding, it will!

This should be of particular concern to all of us since we know that community involvement is important to our own personal growth and the growth of our communities.

Margaret J. Wheatley and Myron Kellner-Rogers in their article "The Paradox and Promise of Community" made some very interesting points concerning our need for community. They explain that, "These systems teach that the instinct of community is not peculiar to humans but is found everywhere in life, from microbes to the most complex species. They also teach that the way in which individuals weave themselves into ecosystems is quite paradoxical."

They explain that individuals and systems arise from two seemingly conflicting forces. These forces are the absolute need for individual freedom and the unequivocal need for relationships. They go on to say:

> *"Individuals cannot survive alone. They move out continuously to discover what relationships they require, what relationships are possible. Evolution progresses from these new relationships, not from the harsh and lonely dynamics of survival of the fittest. Species that decide to ignore relationships that act in greedy and rapacious ways simply die off. If we look at the evolutionary record, it is cooperation that increases over time. This cooperation is spawned from a fundamental recognition that one individual cannot exist without others, that only in relationship can individuals be fully themselves. The instinct of community is everywhere in life."*

In 1977, the well known American cultural anthropologist Margaret Mead told Eric Utne, founder of the Utne Reader, that 99 percent of the time humans have lived on this planet we've lived in groups of 12 to 36 people. Utne stated, "For the full flowering of the human spirit we need groups, tribes, community."

Utne's hope is that some day our children will know the experience of community conveyed by a common phrase of the Xhosa people of southern Africa: "I am because we are." He goes on to say:

> *"There is something about being human that makes us yearn for the company of others, to be with and be touched by our family, friends, and clan. Moving about in the world, stuck inside our own skin, we often feel alone and isolated from the rest of creation."*

Anyone who has experienced being an outsider knows the feeling of loneliness. There is a sense of isolation that is only softened by our connections with others. These connections may be found within our families, workplace, or any of the groups we choose to join. Our connections to people are only limited by our willingness to be accepted by and be accepting of others.

Before the advent of industry, our ancestors knew what it meant to be part of a community. They each had their role, they each played their part. Acceptance by the family and tribe was the natural way of things. The sense of belonging our ancestors enjoyed is difficult to find today.

Arthur E. Morgan in his article, *Homo spiens: The Community Animal*, taken from the book, *In the Company of Others*, explains:

"In modern America, the village, the neighborhood, the hamlet, or the city, often has become but an economic aggregation or only an incidental grouping, without the acquaintance, the personal relationships, and the common interests and activities, which are the essential characteristics of a community. Such aggregations do not fully satisfy the emotional cravings for fellowship, common interests, and unified planning and action."

In the movie "Funny Farm," Chevy Chase plays a Manhattan sportswriter, by the name of Farmer, who abandons his career for life in the country. He is accompanied by his supportive wife, played by Madolyn Smith. His dream, to write the great American novel, changes as dramatically as his surroundings. Her dream becomes evident only as she adjusts to her new surroundings.

The couple comes in contact with a strange assortment of people from the local village of Red Bud. Life doesn't turn out the way they had hoped. The couple's personal relationship ends up at risk, much like their plans for a blissful Norman Rockwellian existence. The not-so-happy couple failed to relate to each other and to their community.

It wasn't until they decided to sell their farm that they realized what the community meant to them. They marketed their farm to another couple in a way that made their lives appear picturesque. The community was one of inclusion. Everyone knew and cared about each other. Greetings were cheeringly passed on the streets. Special attention was given to the needs of neighbors. It was all a deception. The villagers were offered money if they would masquerade as caring neighbors long enough to sell the farm to strangers. It was as though the village wore a mask to hide the nature of what it really was.

This community came together to make money, nothing else. Once the Farmers understood what the community could be, they changed their mind about selling their farm. They stayed in Red Bud, became part of the village and made a place for themselves. They became active participants in community-building. No longer was it acceptable to be passive observers. At some point they must have realized that it was their responsibility to build relationships and become part of the community. Their dreams, although different than their initial plans, were nurtured by the relationships that are, after all, what community is all about.

Building a community takes time and effort. You cannot build relationships or community while living in a self-imposed cocoon. It is easy to spend time in a cubicle or office with only a computer or television for company. But we weren't meant to spend our time away from the company of others. We have an innate desire to be with others, to relate to others, to be part of a community that fulfills our need for belonging and for giving.

SERVICE

"You have not done enough, you have never done enough, so long as it is still possible that you have something to contribute."

—Dag Hammarskjold, Swedish Diplomat and
Second Secretary General of the United Nations

Service is actually about relationships. The great service providers are the people who enter into long lasting and meaningful relationships with others. The individuals who are really great at providing exceptional service are the ones who truly love others.

Without empathy or compassion our attempts at providing service become shallow and meaningless. Humans are intuitive, they can see through hollow attempts at service calculated to meet some prescribed organizational value based initiative. We can tell when someone is being nice because it is time for an annual review. Doing good because you must is not the same as doing good because you want to. Great service providers embody the following characteristics:

- They genuinely like people
- They take action when needed
- They are empathetic
- They want to help
- They anticipate needs
- They take time to listen
- They stay in touch
- They share their feelings
- They are genuine
- They put service before self

Nothing difficult here, right? Wrong! It takes a lot of work to be the type of person who has a reputation for service-based action. When we take time to think about it, who in your organization is the type of person known for their outstanding service? Is it you?

Albert Schweitzer was inspired when he said, "There is no higher religion than human service. To work for the common good is the greatest creed." Doing good by serving the needs of others applies to family, friends, strangers, the environment, and the workplace. We should honor those who willingly serve the needs of others. The best way to honor those who lovingly support the common good is to emulate their actions.

The idea of service-before-self was imaginatively captured by Catherine Ryan Hyde in her novel, *Pay It Forward*. The film version of the novel starred Kevin Spacey, Helen Hunt and Haley Joel Osment. The hero of her story was

Trevor McKinney, a 12-year-old who was given an extra credit assignment in Social Studies. His project was to think of an idea for world change, and put it into action. He decided to do a good deed for three people, and in exchange, he asked each of them to "pay it forward" to three more people.

Trevor's efforts appeared to end in failure but his acts of kindness had long lasting and unanticipated benefits. His service to others, the relationships he created, brought about an entire movement that spread across the America. One child's willingness to make a difference touched many lives.

Those who embody the spirit of service-before-self understand the concept of paying forward. They don't just pay forward three times; they pay forward all the time. They are the relaters, the ones who touch hearts and souls.

> *"When service is relegated to a technique or a program, it becomes nothing more than a sophisticated method of manipulating people to act in ways that accomplish organizational objectives...Service that comes from a pure motive has the power to unite people, bring meaning to their lives, and enrich their humanness. Therein lies genuine happiness and one of the secrets to the spirit of service that distinguishes Southwest Airlines."*
>
> —Kevin & Jackie Freiberg
> *Nuts: Southwest Airlines' Crazy Recipe for Business and Personal Success*

Legendary service is sincere service. The Freibergs explain, *"It's difficult to provide service that is sincere when you operate in an environment that is superficial, cold, and unfriendly."* People do not relate well to this type of environment. People are physical beings who relate to an environment where their emotional, spiritual and psychological needs are met.

Organizations that are attentive to the person behind the need are more likely to establish a long term and mutually beneficial relationship. Relationships are built on trust and people tend to trust those who understand and willingly provide for the needs of others.

Have you ever listened to a speaker or teacher who just read the lines from a well, or not so well, rehearsed script? There was no passion in their presentation because there was no sincerity related to the topic they were addressing. People who love what they do are passionate about their work. If someone isn't passionate about serving others, their insincerity will manifest itself in the way they relate to others.

How many of us like to be manipulated by others? How many of us sense when we are being manipulated? It isn't any fun and is extremely irritating. Yet, there are those who believe it is acceptable to manipulate in order to present a façade of service. True service must be sincere. True service is selfless and action oriented. True service is given with patience and compassion.

It has been my experience that the people who best embody sincere service are kind, generous, and considerate of others. They truly want to be of assistance. They get a rush from being of service and knowing, in some small way, they have made someone's life a little easier.

Mother Teresa embodied the concept of sincere service. Her goal in life was to help others. Her efforts were acknowledged around the world because she sincerely wanted to serve others. She did this quite effectively, one person at a time. There was no manipulation in her actions. She helped everyone she came in contact with in a compassionate and caring way. Her spirit of service was embraced by those who saw it for what it was, a sincere desire to serve those with the greatest need.

Where have you seen someone provide sincere service to you? How did you feel when you knew this person was really interested in helping you? Did you notice their exuberance? Did you acknowledge their heartfelt desire to be of service? Wouldn't it be great if sincere service was the norm rather than an infrequent event?

Sincere service isn't relegated to a technique or program. It isn't about manipulation. Sincere service comes from the purest of intentions and has the power to improve and enrich our lives and all those we serve.

BACK TO SCHOOL

Every year I looked forward to going to open house at our local elementary school, middle school, and high school. It started with my son and daughter's entry into Kindergarten and continued through the end of high school.

As always, the school was jammed full of parents and kids who were anticipating the beginning of a new school year. The floors were scrubbed, the chalkboards were cleaned, and the educators were in their classrooms anxiously awaiting the visiting moms, dads, and kids.

We usually waited impatiently in line with the other families to speak to the teacher(s) who would have such an important influence on the life of our children. In the small community I live in, we already knew a lot about the teachers (seems like everyone is a teacher, a farmer, or both) and they already knew a lot about us, but we still got through the annual "welcome back to school" ceremony.

My mind was put at ease as I saw the enthused teachers and classroom walls papered with motivational statements that embodied the most important lessons we can share with each other. Posters stressed self-empowerment, honesty, caring for others, enthusiasm, team building, and other attributes we all try to instill in our offspring.

There were always many friendly faces to see and hands to shake. The end of the school year temporarily separated friends and the beginning of a new school year brought them back together again. This applied to both parents and students.

I learned that our elementary school principal/Boy Scout troop leader still liked to wear Looney Tune ties. We saw who had grown over the summer and who hadn't.

But what was really powerful was how this whole event allowed the teachers and administrators to kickoff a new school season by showing others their past victories and their vision for the school year that was about to start. Everything pointed towards new beginnings and the energy to make them happen abounded in the bustling halls.

You could see the enthusiasm in the eyes of the educators as they shared their vision for a new year. And since I had come to know many of these people, I knew they were sincere and that they would do their very best for their students.

We should value kickoffs and how we can use them to re-invigorate ourselves and others. Wouldn't it be interesting if businesses had an annual kickoff where we re-commit ourselves to workplace renewal? We could share with others what our most exemplary accomplishments were over the past year and what we hope to accomplish this year. We could also share the values we hold most dear. This should be done by word and by deed, and lots and lots of motivational artwork.

What a perfect way to create a team of individuals that are interested in helping each other. "Oh, you want to improve upon how we communicate? Me too, let's work on this together." Or, "I've been interested in a similar project; maybe we can get others to help us."

Think how effective we could all be if we even took this a step further and decided to partner with dissimilar organizations that have similar concerns. As an example, if you brought together civil servants and educators you would exponentially increase the number of creative ideas that would benefit both groups. This is powerful stuff!

As an example, I was at a meeting where a teacher was given the opportunity to spend a few days with a local for-profit business. She was allowed to attend their leadership training and to participate in some of their business activities. She expressed, with great emotion (we're talking tears here), how this experience was one of the most wonderful opportunities for personal growth she had ever had. She went on to explain that she was going to take back everything she had learned to her students.

What a great way to share with others. There is relatively no cost and a ton of benefits. Maybe we should all commit ourselves to going back to school once a year, at least symbolically.

ACCOUNTABILITY

"You can't expect people to take risks if you continue to insist that they seek approval for every action! You can't craft policies and procedures based on the assumption that people can't be trusted, while at the same time expecting them to use their best judgment and to do the right thing! And you can't dictate policies and at the same time empower people. It just won't work!"

—Rob Lebow & Randy Spitzer
Accountability

There are many definitions of leadership and management. Lebow and Spitzer explain the role of the manager in a very unique way. "A manager is someone who has done such a poor job of hiring that he or she has now got to watch the poor devils on a full-time basis". Ouch!

How much time do you spend watching others? How much time do others spend watching you? The truth is we all resent being controlled. People resist being forced to do anything. We need to find ways to lead people by making them accountable for the outcome of their efforts. And why should we do that? Illuminated leaders understand that people work better when given the freedom to do their jobs.

The old way of managing people is control-based leadership. The new way of managing people is freedom-based leadership. Who hasn't learned that when you control people, they become less responsible and accountable? People can be great, they want to be great, and they even need to be great. But who can be great when they feel controlled and manipulated? We all need the freedom to do our very best, and we won't do our very best unless we have accountability for the outcome of our actions.

Lebow and Spitzer explain that control-based thinking organizations get people to be accountable by imposing authority through hierarchy, direct supervision, quotas and using policies and procedures. They also offer awards through internal competition, incentive plans and appraisal systems. Further, they grant conditional freedom by removing some controls. They empower people to take responsibility without full authority. They even encourage group input without giving them the authority to act. Finally, they have peers scrutinize peers and they create personal improvement plans.

Freedom-based thinking organizations handle things a little differently. They grant individual freedom as a right. They give individuals the freedom to make choices. They ask everyone to be personally responsible. They allow people to design and own their jobs and create their systems. Freedom-based thinking organizations have faith in their people. They believe that everyone wants to be great, and trust them to do great things.

Control based organizations tend to think that people cannot be trusted. They believe that without controls in place, their people will perform poorly and in some cases, take advantage when given the opportunity. Yet Lebow and Spitzer ask some salient questions that point to the need for freedom-based leadership:

> *"But why set up new rules that penalize everyone for the failures or sins of the few? Why build control-based systems to safeguard the operation from the actions of a few untrustworthy people and in the process discourage your most creative people from generating the big wins?"*

These are all tough questions. These questions deserve serious consideration. Let's add two more tough questions to the list: Does control-based leadership ensure accountability? Or do we believe that freedom-based leadership ensures accountability?

When do you feel most accountable for an important job or project? Is it when you feel controlled or when you have the freedom to express your talent, your creativity? And when do you add the greatest value to your organization? When you feel controlled or when you feel free to express yourself?

Freedom-based corporate cultures are learning that the move from control to freedom equates not only to a better place to work but also to real long-term shareholder value and job security. Corporations such as Harley Davidson and Nordstrom understand the value of a freedom-based culture. They and other businesses are divesting themselves of control-based management and embracing freedom-based management.

A good first step toward the creation of a freedom-based culture is to make people accountable. We make people accountable by trusting them to do the right things. Giving trust only after someone has earned it takes forever.

Illuminated leaders give unconditional trust until a person proves themselves to be untrustworthy. Very few will prove to be untrustworthy and the ones that are untrustworthy were that way all along. Most people will earn the trust you give and hold themselves accountable for their actions. By giving unconditional trust, people will be accountable and take the kind of risks we need them to take.

THINK SMALL-TOWN

> *"I've always worried that as people rely more on technology for communicating, particularly e-mail and voice mail, they rely less and*

less on their face-to-face personal skills. And slowly but steadily, those
everyday skills—the common decencies like politeness and sensitivity to
other people's feelings—erode away."

—Mark H. McCormack
Staying Street Smart in the Internet Age

It is easy to forget that the real business of leadership is people. This is particularly true when we realize the advances that have been made in technology. It is tempting to use technology even when we know we would be more effective by walking away from the computer and spending time with our people.

Technology allows us to be connected to others more than ever before and disconnected at the same time. We have improved our communications efficiency at the cost of effective human interactions. The temptation to hide behind technology must be avoided. Technology has its place, but so does face-to-face communication with others. Human contact isn't just smart, it is necessary in order for leaders to know their people and to understand the unique talent they bring into the workplace.

Mark McCormack stresses the need for businesses to treat employees in much the same way you would treat someone in a small town. In a small town you know everyone and so you're held accountable for your behavior. When passing on the street you greet each other and exchange pleasantries. In a small town, if you drive past someone and splash them, you would stop the car and apologize. That isn't necessarily the case in a big town. In a small town, face-to-face communication is expected and politeness is the norm.

McCormack goes on to explain that many businesses act like big towns where you are surrounded by strangers and big-town ways. In his words:

"In my experience, every business is like a small town. The people you deal
with—from the regular customers and clients to the prospects who never
return your phone calls—may seem like strangers, but they are really your
neighbors. And you should behave accordingly. Think twice before you splash
them. And if you splash them, apologize—because they'll remember if you
don't and they in turn will tell their neighbors who'll remember it as well, and
that in turn will come back to haunt you."

Does your workplace feel like a small town or a big town? How do you treat those you work with? Are they treated like strangers or like neighbors? Interestingly enough, I live in a small town so I understand small town culture and the advantages it brings to the workplace. In a small town you know everyone and everyone knows you. You understand the important role each person plays within the community. You know the grocer, postmaster, police officer, school principal, teacher and others. You know their names, you know their family, and you know their interests. Basically, you have a symbiotic relationship with these people.

E-mail, voice mail and other productive technologies are great for communicating efficiently. The Luddites of the world are kidding themselves if they think they can ignore the advantages these tools bring to the workplace. In fact, I would recommend using these and other tools whenever possible to enhance personal productivity. The problem is that many people use technology to avoid the greatest resource available to any leader. That resource is their people. If you think you can successfully lead others strictly through the use of technology and without building meaningful relationships, you are deluding yourself.

Your computer doesn't understand the concept of politeness and sensitivity. Computers don't care about town size. Hanging out with your computer instead of your people is a recipe for relational disaster. Use your computer and other productive tools to enhance your efficiency. Hang out with your people to enhance your personal and organizational effectiveness. Think small-town.

Action plan for service:

- Join clubs and associations. Get involved.
- Be a volunteer.
- Watch less television.
- Get actively involved in your community.
- Serve others with heartfelt sincerity.
- Be kind, generous, and considerate of others.
- Show your enthusiasm.
- Share your unique talents with others.
- Be accountable and trust others to be the same.
- Create a freedom-based culture.
- Think small-town.

Reflective Thoughts

7

Relationships

"Relationships of trust depend on our willingness to look not only to our own interests, but also the interests of others."

—Peter Farquharson

"You do not need to be loved, not at the cost of yourself. The single relationship that is truly central and crucial in a life is the relationship to the self. Of all the people you will know in a lifetime, you are the only one you will never lose."

—Jo Coudert

The illuminated leader brings their unique self into every relationship. They are energized people and like to hang out with other energized people. *Energy vampires*, those who take away energy, are avoided.

Others are allowed to be themselves without losing their unique self. A balance is maintained between meeting personal needs and the needs of others. *Selflessness* is important but must be tempered with attention to one's own needs. Relationship to self is as important as relationship to others.

The illuminated leader takes time to be with *family* and friends. Friends are treated as family, there is no difference. Illuminated leaders appreciate being in the NOW and value every moment they have with others.

Time is taken to learn people's names and the knowledge they have to share. The illuminated leader understands the importance of knowing what is going on in people's lives both inside and outside the work environment. They do this without being intrusive.

Illuminated leaders spend most of their waking hours at work. For this reason they ensure their *time* is spent wisely. Their relationship with time is critical to their success and life balance. They spend time doing what they love and loving what they do.

Illuminated leaders are mentors. A mentor is someone who is both wise and supporting. Mentorship is a very special form of relationship that is most commonly associated with the world of work. Mentors must care about those they support and actively invest in the ongoing development of the protégé.

As mentors they unselfishly impart their wisdom for the benefit of others. They help others learn important lessons that might not have been learned as well, or at all, without assistance. They act as facilitators who impart learning so that others can grow and benefit from their experience. Illuminated leaders are active participants in the planting, nurturing, and harvesting of unlimited human potential.

Organizational *politics* are a reality whether we like it or not. Illuminated leaders understand that any kind of organized human activity involves politics. Illuminated leaders are positive politicians. They understand the value of politics and refuse to lower their ethical standards. Because they interface and relate well with others, illuminated leaders are very successful at organizational politics.

Illuminated leaders know that building relationships is critical to being successful in life. They understand that maintaining meaningful relationships begins with *networking*. Networking is about connecting with others, one person at a time. Everyone has the capacity to connect. It just so happens that illuminated leaders are networking masters.

Finally, illuminated leaders genuinely care about their people and they show it. Their thoughtfulness effectively produces astounding results. They know the time they spend on their people today will pay huge dividends far into the future. Taking time to show they care, to be supportive, is one of the wisest investments any illuminated leader can make.

SELFLESSNESS

"Love is the selfless promotion of the growth of the other."

—Milton Mayeroff
On Caring

"We have a deep need for closeness and unity with others. This need has evolved through millions of years, and will likely be with us to the end of time. Until recently all we required of our relationships was that they provide survival, security, and the continuation of the species. Now

we have added a stiff new requirement: Our relationships must bring
happiness, fulfillment, creativity, and even enlightenment."

—Gay Hendricks & Kathlyn Hendricks
Conscious Loving

Relationships can be the extremely rewarding and infinitely difficult to maintain. We require a great deal from those we look to for companionship. Some of us were lucky enough to be part of a family that was free of mistrust and dissonance. Others were not quite that lucky.

The illuminated leader understands the rewards that come from meaningful relationships. They also understand that the relationships we establish through our work are as important as those established outside of work. The illuminated leader makes the establishment of meaningful relationships a personal goal.

A personal goal of any meaningful relationship should be that of a co-commitment which allows people to be themselves. Bringing our unique self into a relationship should prove advantageous to everyone involved. We should commit ourselves to our own personal growth as well as the growth of others.

The illuminated leader understands it is a mistake to try to control others. In fact, trying to control others should be treated like any other addiction. Healthy relationships exist when we treat others as equals. Drs. Gay Hendrickson and Kathlyn Hendricks explain:

> "In a close relationship, we have two distinct needs: closeness and independence. In a co-committed relationship, both these needs are acknowledged and celebrated. You get close, and when it is time, you separate for a while. Then it's time to go for more closeness. A good relationship is a pulsation of closeness and space...Again, imagine it as a dance. Two people come close, dance together a while, then separate to rest. Both the getting close and the coming apart are essential, because humans are separate beings as well as beings who thrive on union with others...In a healthy relationship, both people are always in the process of noticing what barriers they are putting in the way of meeting these needs."

If we were being honest with ourselves, we'd acknowledge our need for closeness and independence. Sometimes, our need for closeness is not in sync with another's need for independence. Sometimes, the opposite is true.

It takes a leader who is capable of self-monitoring their environment to understand when others seek closeness and support or when they need their independence. In the world of work it is often assumed that closeness isn't allowed, that we must set up barriers in order to be better leaders. This isn't true.

Selflessness is about the promotion of the growth others. To do this effectively we must establish meaningful relationships. Relationships can be difficult to maintain but the rewards make the effort worthwhile. Illuminated leaders understand the importance of selflessness by breaking down barriers and working at establishing relationships that ensure closeness and unity.

ENERGY

"We live in a changing universe where energy constantly flows from one form to another. The seasons teach us there is a time for everything. In the summer the energy flows to produce bountiful harvests and crops. In autumn, the energy of creation slowly leaves the land as it prepares for winter to recharge. Then winter comes and the land in essence hibernates and reenergizes itself. The land stores up and maximizes its energy to get ready to give life once again in the spring. In the springtime, energy flows and creates vibrancy and liveliness that will lead to a fruitful summer. Each season is essential to the other. And each moment in our life is essential to living the next."

—Jon Gordon
Energy Addict

Gordon explains that we all go through cycles in our lives. Some times we feel creative, sometimes we feel reflective. We are often energized while other times we feel drained of energy. Just as the seasons change, so we must also go through periods of high and low energy.

We've learned from science that energy isn't created or destroyed, it just is. As beings of energy, we constantly interact with other forms of energy. Sometimes the interactions are beneficial and sometimes they are hurtful. Have you been around a person or organization that made you feel energized? Have you been around a person or organization that left you feeling totally drained?

Because our energy is limited, we must invest it wisely. Are we spending our energy with people and organizations that move us towards what we care about? If not, we should reconsider whether our energy is being used wisely.

Energy can be found in the words we speak and the words we hear. The opposite of course is also true. Our own words and the words of others can give or take away our energy. Jon Gordon terms those who take energy from us as Energy Vampires. Do Energy Vampires exist in the real world? Of course they do, and you don't have to travel to Transylvania to find them. They are all around us.

According to Gordon, "They lurk in our businesses, our families, and our social organizations. They are real. They are everywhere. And they will suck the life out of you if you let them." Energy Vampires don't use fangs to steal your energy, what they do is much more insidious.

One sure sign of an Energy Vampire is their constant negative comments. Nothing is ever good enough. No one listens to them and everyone is out to get them. Their very presence in a room is enough to zap our strength.

Another sign is someone who refuses to believe in your dreams. Rather than support your efforts they will find fault with all you do or hope to do. The word "can't" is forever etched into their vocabulary. These people will spend hours researching why something can't be done rather than perceiving the possibility of a positive outcome.

Finally, an Energy Vampire is an expert at finding fault and blame in others. They will do whatever it takes to put you down in order to validate their own negativity. They are experts at the blame-game.

Gordon suggests some actions steps we might take when we come face-to-face with an Energy Vampire. One step is to ensure we aren't Energy Vampires. Are we negative or positive? By paying attention to our own thoughts, we can be a positive influence on others and give energy rather than take it away. You can't be both positive and negative at the same time. I've found being positive much more fun than being negative. In fact, when we look for what is positive in our life, we tend to find more of it.

He also suggests we confront and reform those who are negative. It could be they don't realize the draining impact they have on others. We can honestly ask them for their support and encouragement. If we have an abundance of kindness and positive energy, we can put it to good use to help someone who is willing to change.

Of course, there are those who are so invested in their own negativity they are unwilling to change. Their personalities are so intertwined with their negativism; the very idea of being positive is a totally foreign concept. These people will drain you of energy every chance they get. Sometimes it is better to cut your losses and spend your time and energy where you can focus on what matters most in your life.

Just like the seasons, your energy will ebb and flow. You will have times of vibrancy and times when you need to re-energize. The people and organizations you spend time with will have a direct impact on your energy level. Hang around people and organizations that give you energy. Avoid people and organizations, if possible, who take energy from you. Use your energy wisely and remember; you can't be positive and negative at the same time, so choose to be positive.

THE KILLER APP

According to Tim Sanders, *Love is the Killer App*, the most important new trend in business is the downfall of the barracudas, sharks, and piranhas, and the ascendancy of nice, smart people. Sanders definition of love as it relates to business associates is *"the act of intelligently and sensibly sharing your intangibles with your bizpartners."* To Sanders, the intangibles are knowledge, networks, and compassion. His list makes sense when you think about it.

We spend an inordinate amount of time at work. We come in contact with dozens of business associates every day. How many of our associates do we really know? How many of them really know us? Have we even taken the time to learn their names, or the knowledge they have to share? What is going on in their lives both inside and outside the work environment that has an impact on how we do business?

Before remarkable technological advances took place in business, people could retain value for long periods of time without undergoing radical personal change. Today, this is not the case. The net worth of an advanced degree seems to depreciate at about the same rate as a computer or automobile. The books you read in order to stay knowledgeable in your field of expertise are 2-3 years old before they ever reach a bookstore. So how do we stay knowledgeable when what was taken for granted yesterday doesn't work anymore?

One suggestion is to increase our knowledge. We can do this by becoming a book-reading zealot. Read constantly and share what you have learned with others. A passion for reading pays great dividends both personally and organizationally. A great way to build solid relationships with business associates is to share what you've learned from a book or book on tape/disk. "Jennifer, remember the orientation program you were working on? I just read this great book about a program that has been very successful, would you like to hear about it?"

The more you read, the more you have to offer others in the way of sage advice. The more you share with others, the more knowledge you will receive from them in return. Sharing knowledge is a way to show interest in others. One thoughtful comment will lead to others. A relationship is built one small step at a time. The person you may least suspect of some hidden talent may be a world-class musician or hobbyist who will generously share their knowledge if asked. What we don't know about others can hurt us, or at least can't help us.

Another way to gain knowledge is to join a book club or discussion group. This is an opportune way to meet others who share similar interests. By joining this type of group you gain knowledge and gain a valuable network of associates.

Networking is now as important for people as it is for computers. We need to stay connected with those we like and with those we need. Hanging out with the computer all day may be someone's idea of fun but it doesn't guarantee success in a business world that demands we constantly add value. Today, more than ever, our value is enhanced by our relationship with others.

Networking is also an effective way to grow relationships.

What clubs do you belong to? If you aren't connected to others through clubs or associations, now would be a good time to start. Physical location is no longer an excuse to be disconnected from others. Discussion groups exist for nearly every interest a person can imagine. If you are the sole person in Human Resources or Training and Development for a firm, you can seek or share the wisdom of the ages through the Internet. Knowledge and meaningful relationships are only a mouse click away for those willing to share their experiences with others.

According to Jaymes Song of the Associated Press, Kent M. Keith wrote the following 10 maxims at the age of 19, in his dormitory at Harvard, and included them in a 65 page booklet published for high school student leaders:

- People are illogical, unreasonable and self-centered. Love them anyway.
- If you do good, people will accuse you of selfish ulterior motives. Do good anyway.
- If you are successful, you win false friends and true enemies. Succeed anyway.
- The good you do today will be forgotten tomorrow. Do good anyway.
- Honesty and frankness make you vulnerable. Be honest and frank anyway.
- The biggest men and women with the biggest ideas can be shot down by the smallest men and women with the smallest minds. Think big anyway.
- People favor underdogs but follow only top dogs. Fight for a few underdogs anyway.
- What you spend years building may be destroyed overnight. Build anyway.
- People really need help but may attack you if you do help them. Help people anyway.
- Give the world the best you have and you'll get kicked in the teeth. Give the world the best you have anyway.

The thoughtful, relationship-oriented person in an organization may not always be the one with the most important title on the door or the one who dominates meetings. They may not even be the person to whom others turn for action. But in every successful organization there is at least one person who is oriented toward relationships and who guides others. The official leader does well to identify and encourage this person.

The official leader in any organization should understand and apply the killer applications of knowledge, networks, and compassion. When these applications are used properly the official leader becomes an illuminated leader.

TIME

"We all learned in Philosophy 101 that time doesn't really exist…it's just a convenient convention, concocted eons ago to make life predictable. In many ways, the concept of business time is under radical overhaul. Winning organizations are sure to be those that use time (or the lack of it) as their ally."

—Chip R. Bell & Oren Harari
Beep! Beep!

At the beginning of each school year we can almost hear a communal sigh of relief from parents as they plan on sending their kids back to our bastions of education. As a kid (about a million years ago) this meant an exciting time of buying new clothes and school supplies with both a sense of dread and excitement. The excitement centered on seeing friends that somehow became disconnected over the long weeks of summer vacation. The dread had to do with the uncertainty of a new school year.

I think it must be a similar experience for my kids. We've certainly visited the crowded stores, checking off the school supplies on our list as we vied for tablets, notebooks, and even a dwindling supply of scientific calculators.

It seemed a lot easier when I went through the *going back to school ceremony*. Everything I needed was purchased at basically one store. There were no designer clothes or even designer tablets, or pencils for that matter.

I didn't understand the importance of designer clothes and logos then but now it's all I see. It can be confusing, and I'm pretty sure I may have experienced a slight heart palpitation when I saw the price tag on a pair of shoes that carried that sacred Nike logo.

But once we get through the *going back to school ceremony* we are faced with even bigger challenges. How to get one or more kids to one or more functions at more than one location and generally at exactly the same time?

My daughter Fleming use to have volleyball, band, girl scouts, and music lessons. Sage still has soccer, tennis, 4H, choir, band, and much more. Thank goodness his mom has her chauffeur's license.

Cindy and I stretch our time management skills to the limit. There are plays, open houses, meetings with teachers, last minute events, and a host of activities that would send chills down the spine of any time management expert.

I have taught time management and I have to admit that there is a lot of wisdom in following Dr. Stephen Covey's concept of putting *first things first*. And if there was ever a time to use that concept it is right about now.

Illuminated leaders understand when putting first things first, families should be on the top of the list. That doesn't mean that we can drop everything we're doing every time a family event or need arises. We live in the real world. In the real world there are projects to complete and deadlines to meet.

We need to keep family in our minds and in our hearts. We've all missed some special family events in our lives. Hopefully, there have been some very special moments we haven't missed.

Illuminated leaders understand the time they spend with family is important. The time they spend at work and how they spend their time at work is also extremely important. Julie Morgenstern, *Never Check Your E-Mail in the Morning*, shares some important thoughts worth heeding:

> *"Happiness at work involves liking what you're doing and being good at it—feeling appreciated, in control, successful, and in balance. When you get your work done, or at least conquer your most important tasks, you finish your day with a victorious sense of accomplishment. When you leave the office on time, and not three hours into your family's evening, or after breaking plans to go out with friends, you feel in control."*

We have a relationship with our work just like we do with our family. We spend most of our waking hours at work. For this reason alone, we must ensure our time is spent both wisely and on the right tasks. Top performers are hard-wired into their organization's mission and vision. They ensure the time they spend meets their organization's goals.

Much of the satisfaction we receive at work is from achieving the organization's stated purpose through the attainment of goals. One effective way to attain goals is through organizing skills. To organize properly we must determine what needs to be done, how it must be done, and who will complete the task(s).

As we take on greater management responsibilities, the time we spend on organizing increases. According to Mahoney, Jerdee, and Caroll, *The Job(s) of Management*, first-level managers spend 24 percent of their time organizing, middle-managers spend 33 percent and top-managers spend 36 percent on organizing activities. If you spend 24 to 36 percent of your time organizing, it makes sense to do it efficiently and effectively.

When we are organized we feel in control. Employers love it when we accomplish meaningful goals. We experience the rush that comes after checking items off of our to-do-list. Being organized is critical to our long term success. Yet many succumb to the fast paced tempo at work largely because they haven't truly mastered how to be organized.

One of the key tasks needed to get organized is to create a master-task-list. It is very distracting to have multiple task lists. If you have post-it-notes and slips of paper tucked away where you may or may not find them, it is time for a change. One of the most powerful organizing action items you can and must do is to centralize your task list.

Begin by gathering all of your existing task-list items and consolidate them into one master-task-list. A master-task-list allows you to identify start and completion dates, prioritize taskings, and assign responsibility and much more. I would recommend some effective time management software. If that doesn't work for you, use a personal planner or a piece of paper. After you consolidate your task-list items, take some time for personal reflection and jot down all of the tasks you have been thinking about but haven't written down anywhere.

Every time you think of something you should do, add it to your master-task-list. By placing your tasks on one comprehensive master-list you reduce stress just by knowing you have organized, and can find, all your tasks in one place.

It is important when you create your master-task-list to include tasks relating to all the roles in your life. Life isn't just about work. Be sure to include tasks associated with friends, family, hobbies, and all those things that bring balance into your life. Everyone's idea of balance is unique. A master-task-list that only includes work related tasks will not ensure a balanced life.

Sometimes, work comes first. Sometimes, our personal needs must come first. If you find yourself overly stressed there is a good chance your life is out of balance. If that is the case, take a close look at your master-task-list and re-assess where and what you are spending time on. If you ensure your time is well spent, you will be healthier, happier and in control.

Illuminated leaders, those who achieve the greatest results, tend to have a healthy and balanced relationship with work and life. They consistently give their best while keeping their lives in balance. They master their time wisely.

MENTORSHIP

The word 'mentor' comes from "The Odyssey" written by the ancient Greek poet Homer. In this classic tale, Odysseus leaves to fight in the Trojan War. Before he departs for the war he entrusts the education and well-being of his son and heir Telemachus, to his wise friend Mentor. Odysseus must have fretted over who would have the character traits to ensure his son would someday become a wise ruler. The list of traits he would have valued would be similar to what we all look for in a mentor. According to Chip R. Bell in *Managers as Mentors:*

"The mentor is a teacher, a guide, a sage, and foremost a person acting to the best of his or her ability, in a whole and compassionate way in plain view of the protégé. No greater helping or healing can occur than that induced by a model of compassion and authenticity. Mentoring is about being real, being a catalyst, and being sometimes a kind of prophet."

Illuminated leaders are mentors to others. They understand the value of mentorship and act as mentors while encouraging their followers to do the same. They know that mentorship is one of the most effective ways to create a dynamic workforce.

What is a mentor? A mentor is someone who is both wise and supporting. Mentorship is a very special form of relationship that is most commonly associated with the world of work. Mentors must care about those they support and actively invest in the ongoing development of the protégé.

During our lives, we learn from many different people. It is the mentor who unselfishly imparts their wisdom for the benefit of others. Mentors help others learn important lessons that might not have been learned as well, or at all, without assistance. When we mentor someone, we focus all of our attention on that unique and special person. We become a facilitator who imparts learning so that others can grow and benefit from our experience.

The mentor helps unlock the potential of the protégé through the process of nurturing potential growth. It is through growth that we discover our own greatness and the greatness of others. Mentors are active participants in the planting, nurturing, and harvesting of unlimited human potential.

Great mentors are emotionally involved in the development of protégés. Barriers are lowered so that true dialogue can take place. The relationship between the mentor and protégé is one of openness and mutual respect. The mentor must have the best interest of the protégé at heart so that trust can develop. Chip Bell explains:

"We protect ourselves with the shield of personality (the Greek word for 'personality' means 'mask') and assume that each new relationship is a threat until shown otherwise. The ritual of relationship is the gradual lowering of the mask."

Once the mask is lowered we present ourselves as authentic, caring human beings. This atmosphere opens a path for dialogue. When engaged in dialogue, the mentor creates an environment that is comfortable and safe for the protégé. This is an environment where listening and honesty are encouraged.

The mentor can be seen as a gift giver, someone who understands the concept of selflessness. They give their time and wisdom without thought of reward. The reward comes in knowing someone has been helped and that a connection has been created. The mentor takes pride in the accomplishments of their protégé and encourages their ongoing development.

Illuminated leaders embrace mentorship because they understand the value it brings to their organization. Illuminated leaders are mentors to others and they enthusiastically encourage a culture of mentorship.

POSITIVE POLITICS

> *"The person who scorns organizational politics usually does not understand that he or she continually participates in a political contest, willingly or unwillingly, consciously or unconsciously. If you work for an organization or participate in any kind of organized human activity, you've involved yourself in its politics. Declaring yourself out of the game doesn't get you out of the game. You can't not play – you can only play competently or incompetently."*

—Karl Albrecht
Social Intelligence

How often have we heard someone say, "I don't play office politics" or "The only way to get ahead around here is to play politics." Usually their tone of voice reflects disapproval or condemnation for those who do play the political game at work. The truth is, we are all involved in politics whether we care to admit it or not. Realistically, how we interface and relate to others will determine how successful we are at organizational politics.

Politics has earned a bad reputation and is often seen only for the negative connotations associated with the term. We've all known or heard of those who reflect the worst behaviors associated with politics. There are those who find lying, cheating, deceiving, back-stabbing, selfishness and worse, acceptable behaviors for getting ahead in an organization. Unfortunately these tactics do sometimes work, however; the price is not worth the long term costs.

Just because some people opt to play the political game with low moral standards does not mean the rest of us have to follow along in order to compete effectively for promotions and influence. A high moral code of ethics is a much better way to gain life's rewards while maintaining the political high-ground.

Anyone who believes they are not involved in politics is delusional. We are all involved and impacted by politics. How often and how effectively we choose to be involved is a personal choice. The political process will go on with or without conscious participation. Political passivity is a path that allows others to receive the promotions, influence, and rewards that we might receive if we actively engage in ethical politic behavior.

Politics can be defined as interactions between people where we seek to influence one another. We all know that there are those who influence solely for their own self-interest. This is a personal choice. We also know there are those who influence for honorable and less selfish reasons. This is also a personal choice.

Over the years I have worked for, worked with, and have been influenced by those who have used both positive and negative politics in the workplace. I'm glad to say that those who assert themselves positively tend to receive the long-term promotions and rewards rather than their negative counterparts. I've also noted that those who use positive politics in the workplace are almost always focused on their organizations mission rather than personal self-interest. This only goes to prove that there is justice in the world.

Everyone can choose to be a positive politician. Positive politicians exert influence that is beneficial to the individual and the organization. Karl Albrecht in his book, *Personal Power: Knowing What You Want, Getting What You Want*, identifies ten skills of positive politics. These skills include:

- Do something well; get recognized as an achiever
- Form alliances and service them regularly
- Get visibility
- Get credit for your achievements
- Relieve pain when possible
- Contribute to the big picture
- Keep developing yourself
- Have a plan for your progress in the organization
- Have options to your current job—especially in good times
- Know when to leave

Scorning politics is an exercise in futility. Passively observing organizational politics lessens the likelihood of promotions and rewards. Negative politics may work temporarily, but the final cost is not worth the pain and suffering it causes. Positive politics benefits both the individual and the organization. We're all involved in politics, so we might as well deal with it as competently and honorably as possible. The best choice is to get into the game by willingly being a positive influence in your organization.

NETWORKING

"Relationships are all there is. Everything in the universe only exists because it is in relationship to everything else. Nothing exists in isolation. We have to stop pretending we are individuals that can go it alone."

—Margaret Wheatley
Consultant and Speaker

Rugged individualism is dead, long live networking! Relationship building begins with networking. Keith Ferrazzi in his book, *Never Eat Alone*, said he learned that real networking was about finding ways to make other people more successful. It was about working hard to give more than you get. It sounds somewhat biblical.

Illuminated leaders know that building relationships is critical to being successful in life. Whether we're focused on a career, family or friends, establishing and maintaining meaningful relationships begins with networking. In reality, networking is nothing more than connecting with others, one person at a time. Everyone has the capacity to connect. It just so happens that some people are better at it than others.

Why do we need to connect with others? Ferrazi explains:

"Connecting—with the support, flexibility, and opportunities for self-development that come along with it—happens to make a great deal of sense in our new work world. The loyalty and security once offered by organizations can be provided by our own networks. Lifetime corporate employment is dead; we're all free agents now, managing our own careers across multiple jobs and companies. And because today's primary currency is information, a wide-reaching network is one of the surest ways to become and remain thought leaders of our respective fields."

We might be amazed to learn how many people we are already connected with. If we consider family, friends, colleagues, neighbors, former teachers, co-workers, bosses, subordinates, and others, we probably have an impressive list of those we already have a relationship with. These individuals have their own connections and can add their contacts to our network.

Networking requires that we reach out to others. Isolation is not an option if we want to establish meaningful relationships. Attending conferences, meetings, events, and social gatherings are all part of networking and connecting with others. The opportunities to attend and participate in all these activities are nearly limitless, yet, on average, very few people truly take advantage of these important networking events.

Our calendars should be filled with opportunities for meeting new and interesting people. Conferences alone provide a great opportunity to extend professional networks. The same holds true for participation on committees, councils, volunteer organizations, clubs, and other functions where we can socially interact with others.

Networking can be intimidating. For some, networking seems like play, but for the rest of humanity it is hard work. But hard work, in the end, pays off. If networking makes you feel uncomfortable, just remember that you are not alone. The best advice is to work through feelings of fear and rejection and to confidently step out and meet others. Remember to be yourself when meeting someone new and to take time to listen. Studies continually show that those who confidently make conversation with anyone in any situation are more likely to be successful. Just like any other skill, practice makes perfect. Networking is no exception to this rule.

After meeting someone new, consider adding them to your list of future contacts. Without follow-up there can be no relationship. It is through phone-calls, emails, meetings, and other forms of ongoing communication that networking evolves into a relationship. And how important are relationships? Here is what the Dalai Lama has to say:

> *"We human beings are social beings. We come into the world as the result of others' actions. We survive here in dependence on others. Whether we like it or not, there is hardly a moment of our lives when we do not benefit from others' activities. For this reason, it is hardly surprising that most of our happiness arises in the context of our relationships with others."*

Rugged individualism was the norm a century ago. Today we must work to connect with others if we want to be successful in business and as leaders. Success is as much about whom we know as what we know. Networking is no longer an option, and it is a requirement for establishing and building relationships.

CARING

> *"The correlation between not feeling cared about and resigning has been observed repeatedly in studies of individual companies in the Gallup database and in analyses where data from many organizations are combined...Anthropologists see people today as the descendants of the most cooperative humans living across time. In the rugged past, people who didn't work together didn't just have a bad day at work—they died."*
>
> —Rodd Wagner & James K. Harter
> *The 12 Elements of Great Managing*

The workplace today can be compared to the tribes of the past. Why is that? A tribe is basically a group of people sharing a common culture made up of customs, myths, legends, stories, symbols, values, beliefs, rituals, rites and ceremonies. A tribe has the same heroes and heroines. Sounds a lot like today's world of work. Organizations are in a sense modern day tribes that share these same important cultural characteristics.

People have many needs. Wagner and Harter identified a particularly important common need as the fifth element of great managing. The fifth element of great managing is "someone at work cares about me as a person."

This need to feel cared for has a huge impact on organizations today. Lifetime employment went away just like the tribes of old, yet people join and leave tribes/organizations everyday and just like in the past, they have the same basic need as their ancestors, the need to feel that someone at work cares about them.

Leaders who understand the needs of their people are greatly empowered. Leaders who do not understand are disempowered and are often bewildered when they see a lack of commitment in the workplace. You can almost hear the leader say, "why aren't my people more motivated, self-sacrificing, willing to do whatever it takes to support the needs of the organization?" It is better to ask, "What have I done recently to create an environment where my people are motivated, willing to make personal sacrifices and to support the organization?"

Many leaders are amazed when they see their people leave their organization. They ask, "Did they leave for more pay?", or "why is it so hard to retain good people?" In reality, people often leave because they don't feel cared about.

There are many forms of leadership. One very effective form of leadership is categorized as "Supportive Leadership." The supportive leader cares about their people. They know what is going on with their people and they do what they can to have a positive impact on each and every person they supervise. One of the smartest and most effective things any leader can do is to show others how much they care.

It takes time to show you care, yet; if you genuinely care about your people, your efforts can produce astounding results. Supportive leaders know that the time they spend on their people today will pay huge dividends far into the future. Taking time to show you care is a wise investment.

There are many ways to show you care. Some ways include: being friendly (smile), kind, cheerful, gracious, caring, and courteous to others. Some other ideas are to listen carefully, learn names, share your experiences with others, and ask others about their opinions.

Showing others you care is really about establishing a personal relationship, one person at a time. Close personal relationships, where followers feel their leader cares about them, trumps organizational turnover every time, therefore; take time to show you care. Mary Kay Ash, founder of Mary Kay Ash Cosmetics, Inc., understood this concept when she said, "Pretend that every single person you meet has a sign around his or her neck that says, make me feel important."

Action plan for relationships:

- Bring your own unique self into every relationship.
- Be a positive influence on others.
- Hang around people who give you energy.
- Avoid energy vampires.
- Spend time with friends and family.
- Become a book-reading zealot.
- Join a club or discussion group.
- Put first things first.
- Create and use a master-task-list.
- Be a mentor to others.
- Be a positive politician.
- Network-Network-Network
- Practice supportive leadership.
- Make others feel important.

Reflective Thoughts

Summary

In this book you learned that the illuminated leader generates a very special kind of light. You learned that the light generated by illuminated leaders is filled with radiant knowledge, compassion, energy and enthusiasm. Illuminated leaders glory in the accomplishment of others and are the selfless care givers who transform people, cultures, organizations, and even nations.

Through illumination you now know we become resplendent and illustrious. To be an illuminated leader you must model leadership behaviors and traits designed to specifically affect the enlightenment of others. The behaviors and traits addressed in this book included *courage, transformation, communication, character, inspiration, service and relationships.*

Action plans were included with each of the behaviors allowing you to practice the traits needed for illuminated leadership. The list of traits are by no means exhaustive and I encourage you to add any traits to the list you feel will make you a more effective leader.

You now know that illuminated leaders are the torch bearers of enlightened leadership. The light they produce is positive energy made visible. They serve as beacons of excellence enlightening others so they can achieve their own unique brilliance.

Illuminated leaders share their own light and use it to brighten the world. Share your light with the world and always strive to be an illuminated leader.

Bibliography

Albrecht, Karl (2006). Social Intelligence: The New Science of Success. San Francisco: Jossey-Bass.

Axelrod, Alan (2006). Eisenhower on Leadership: Ike's Enduring Lessons in Total Victory Management. San Francisco: Jossey-Bass.

Baum, Frank L. (1900). The Wizard of Oz. New York: Puffin Books

Bell, Chip R. (2002). Managers as Mentors: Building Partnerships for Learning. San Francisco: Berrett Koehler.

Bell, Chip R. & Harari, Oren (2000). Beep! Beep! Competing in the Age of the Road Runner. New York: Warner Books.

Bennis, Warren & Nanus, Burt (2003). Leaders: Strategies for Taking Charge. New York: Harper Collins. New York: Vintage Books.

Bernstein, Frances (2000). Classical Living: Reconnecting with the Rituals of Ancient Rome. San Francisco: Harper.

Bok, Sissela (1999). Lying: Moral Choice in Public and Private Life.

Covey, Stephen M.R. (2007). The Speed of Trust: The One Thing That Changes Everything. New York: Free Press.

Covey, Stephen R. (2004). The 8th Habit: From Effectiveness to Greatness. New York: Free Press.

Csikszentmihalyi, Mihaly (1990). Flow: The Psychology of Optimal Experience. New York: HarperCollins.

Domar, Alice D., & Dreher, Henry (2001). Self Nurture: Learning to Care for Yourself as Effectively as You Care for Everyone Else. New York: Penguin.

Ferrazzi, Keith (2005). Never Eat Alone: And Other Secrets to Success, One Relationship at a Time. New York: Doubleday

Freiberg, Kevin & Kathy (1996). Nuts: Southwest Airlines' Crazy Recipe for Business and Personal Success. New York: Broadway Books.

Freiberg, Kevin & Kathy (2004). Guts: Companies that Blow the Doors Off Business-as-Usual. Doubleday: New York.

Goleman, Daniel, Boyatzis, Richard & McGee, Annie (2004). Primal Leadership: Learning to Lead with Emotional Intelligence. Harvard Business School Press: Boston

Gordon, Jon (2003). Energy Addict: 101 Physical, Mental, & Spiritual Ways to Energize Your Life. The Berkley Publishing Group: New York.

Gostick, Adrian & Elton, Chester (2007). The Carrot Principle: How the Best Managers Use Recognition to Engage Their People, Retain Talent, and Accelerate Performance. Free Press: New York.

Gross, Ronald (2002). Socrates' Way: Seven Master Keys to Using Your Mind to the Utmost. New York: Putnam.

Hansen, Morten T., Nohria, Nitin & Tierney, Thomas (March-April 1999). What's Your Strategy for Managing Knowledge? Boston: Harvard Business Review.

Haskell, Robert (2001). Deep Listening: Hidden Meanings in Everyday Conversation. Cambridge, Massachusetts: Perseus Publishing

Hendricks, Gay., & Ludeman, Kate (1996). The Corporate Mystic: A Guidebook for Visionaries With Their Feet on the Ground. New York: Bantam Books.

Hesselbein, Frances, Goldsmith, Marshall & Beckhard, Richard (1996). The Leader of the Future. New York: The Peter F. Drucker Foundation for Nonprofit Management.

Isaacs, William (1999). Dialogue and the Art of Thinking Together: A Pioneering Approach to Communicating in Business and in Life. New York: Currency.

Jamison, Kay Redfield (2004). Exuberance: The Passion for Life. New York: Random House.

Kanter, Rosabeth Moss (1989). When Giants Learn to Dance: The Definitive Guide to Corporate Amerca's Changing Strategies for Success. New York: Simon & Schuster.

Kanter, Rosabeth Moss (May-June 1999). From Spare Change to Real Change: The Social Sector as Beta Site for Business Innovation. Harvard Business Review. (122-132)

Kiernan, Matthew J. (1996). The Eleven Commandments of 21st Century Management. Englewood Cliffs, NJ: Prentice Hall.

Kotter, John P. (1996). Leading Change. Boston: Harvard Business Press.

Lebow, Rob & Randy Spitzer (2002). Accountability: Freedom and Responsibility Without Control. San Francisco: Berrett-Koehler Publishers Inc.

Loehr, Jim and Schwartz, Tony (2003). The Power of Full Engagement: Managing Energy, Not Time, Is the Key to High Performance and Personal Renewal. New York: Free Press.

McCormack, Mark H. (2000). Staying Street Smart in the Internet Age: What Hasn't Changed About the Way We Do Business. Penguin Putnam Inc., New York.

Mahoney, T.A., Jerdee, T.H., and Carroll, S.J. (1965). The Job(s) of Management. Industrial Relations 4, no. 2, p.103

Morgan, A. (1993). Homo Sapiens: The Community Animal. In the Company of Others: Making Community in the Modern World. New York: Putnam Publishing Group.

Morgenstern, Julie (2005). <u>Never Check E-Mail in the Morning: And Other Unexpected Strategies for Making Your Work Life Work.</u> New York: Simon & Schuster

Pfeffer, Jeffrey & Sutton, Robert I. (May-June 1999). <u>The Smart-Talk Trap.</u> Harvard Business Review. (135-142).
Peters, Tom (1997). <u>The Circle of Innovation.</u> New York: Alfred A. Knopf, Inc.

Peters, Tom (2003). <u>Re-Imagine: Business Excellence in a Disruptive Age.</u> New York: Dorling Kindersley Limited.

Putnam, Robert (1999). <u>The Strange Disappearance of Civic America.</u> The American Prospect no. 24, Winter 1996.

Roger, John & McWilliams, Peter (1991). <u>Do It! Let's Get Off Our Buts.</u> Los Angeles: Prelude Press.

Sanders, Tim (2002). <u>Love is the Killer App: How to Win Business and Influence Friends.</u> New York: Random House Inc.

Secretan, Lance (2004). <u>Inspire! What Great Leaders Do.</u> Hoboken, New Jersey: John Wiley & Sons.

Senge, Peter M. (1990). <u>The Fifth Discipline: The Art & Practice of The Learning Organization.</u> New York: Doubleday Currency.

Senn, Larry E. & Childress, John R. (1999). <u>The Secret of a Winning Culture: Building High-Performance Teams.</u> Leadership Press.

Song, Jaymes, Associated Press, The Columbus Dispatch, March 22, 2002.

Tannen, Deborah (1994). <u>Talking From 9 To 5: How Women's and Men's Conversational Styles Affect Who Gets Heard, Who Gets Credit, And What Gets Done At Work.</u> New York: William Morrow and Company.

Tolle, Eckhart (1999). <u>The Power of Now: A Guide to Spiritual Enlightenment.</u> Vancouver, B.C., Canada. Namaste Publishing.

Thomas, Bob (1994). <u>Walt Disney: An American Original.</u> New York: Hyperion.

Ulrich, Dave (1996). <u>Credibility x Capability. The Leader of the Future.</u> New York: The Peter Fl Drucker Foundation for Nonprofit Management.

Utne, Eric (September 1992). <u>Utne Reader.</u> Minneapolis, Minnesota

Wagner, Rodd & Harter, James K., Ph.D., (2006). <u>The 12 elements of Great Managing.</u> New York: Gallup Press.

Wheatley, Margaret J. (2002). <u>Turning to One Another: Simple Conversations to Restore Hope to the Future.</u> San Francisco: Berrett-Koehler Publishers.

Wheatley, Margaret & Kellner-Rogers, Myron (1998). <u>The Paradox and Promise of Community in the Community of the Future.</u> San Francisco: Jossey-Bass.

Whitmyer, Claude (1993). <u>In the Company of Others: Making Community in the Modern World.</u> New York: Putnam Publishing Group.

Williamson, Marianne (1992). <u>A Return to Love: Reflections on the Principles of a Course in Miracles</u>. New York: Harper Collins.

www.ingramcontent.com/pod-product-compliance
Lightning Source LLC
Chambersburg PA
CBHW030746180526
45163CB00003B/932